ADVANCE ACCLAIM FOR *THE CURVE AHEAD*

"*The Curve Ahead* is a unique book that focuses on the growth challenges of mid-sized companies. Dave Power draws on a lifetime of experiences to show growth company leaders how to sustain growth over time by building innovation into the rhythm of business operations."

—*Eric Schmidt, Executive Chairman of Google*

"The only thing that matters in business is growth and any company that stops growing is dead—particularly if you are a small or mid-size company. Dave has done an excellent job of explaining how and what others have done to sustain growth for the long term. For those who don't want to read a dozen books on growing their business, *The Curve Ahead* is a great, easy to read primer on thinking about how to grow a business."

—*Omar Hussain, President and CEO of Imprivata, Inc.*

"*The Curve Ahead* should be a guidance system for all entrepreneurs who have seen early success but must now scale their company to fulfill their original dreams. Dave has worked with several of my portfolio companies and I have seen how his approach can produce powerful, measurable, and lasting results."

—*Larry Bohn, Managing Director of General Catalyst Partners*

"This book offers great practical guidance and case studies to the CEO who set out to build a fast growth company and discovers that the engine that fueled early stage rocket ship growth is slowing down. A must-read for discovering how to power up the innovation that launched the company so that a company can discover its next curve for growth."

—*Janet Kraus, CEO of Peach Underneath, and
Senior Lecturer at Harvard Business School*

"If you want your business to grow and stay relevant, the first step is to Just Listen to your customers. This is the timeless message of *The Curve Ahead*, a unique book about innovation and growth strategy for mid-size companies."

—*Mark Goulston, bestselling author of* Just Listen

"*The Curve Ahead* brings into sharp focus the innovation process we practice every day at Continuum; combining analytical rigor of business logic and design thinking to uncover people-centric opportunities and then translating such insights into compelling new product and service experiences. Power clearly illustrates a proven process that, by leveraging the individual skill sets and creative sensibilities of interdisciplinary teams to learn what really matters to people, and then conceptualizing, prototyping, testing and refining new and ever more compelling product and service innovations, leaders can reinvigorate and ultimately revolutionize any business or organization by improving the quality of life of the people they serve."

—*Gianfranco Zaccai, President and Chief Design Officer of Continuum LLC*

"*The Curve Ahead* lays out a powerful framework for creating sustainable growth . . . [Dave] Power draws on a 25-year career as an executive, investor and advisor to growth businesses to provide a thoughtful and compelling roadmap for growth company managers confronting the challenge of driving new growth opportunities!"

—John G. Hayes, Great Hill Partners

"The journey from success to sustainable success does indeed require a complete rethink of your business and unlike your past, new products and services will not get you there alone. You must listen to your customers and follow them into new market spaces. Doing this well allows you to bridge together a series of S-curves that can carry you for decades. *The Curve Ahead* is a must read for those trying to get unstuck so you can reach the next level."

—Hunt Lambert, Dean of Harvard Division of Continuing Education and University Extension

"For Entrepreneurs: read *The Curve Ahead* to make sure your growth strategy outlives your current business model."

—David Skok, General Partner of Matrix Partners

"While plenty of business books focus on the entrepreneurial start or the big exit, *The Curve Ahead* examines what is possibly the hardest challenge executives face: sustainable growth. Power offers powerful and pragmatic advice on how to integrate innovation into the lifeblood of a business."

—Meg O'Leary, Cofounder of Inkhouse

"Every successful company will, at some point, come face-to-face with the opportunities, challenges and dynamics of the S-Curve. *The Curve Ahead* has been instrumental in helping Ping Identity understand and improve our innovation strategy for growth."

—Andre Durand, CEO of Ping Identity

"*The Curve Ahead* exposes one of the weaknesses we often see in mid-market growth companies worldwide: No systematic process to create new offers (products, services, or business model innovation) to fuel growth 3 to 5 years into the company's future. Dave draws on his experience as a CEO and Venture Capitalist and astuteness as a Marketing professional to guide leaders in creating an innovation rhythm in their companies."

—Keith Cupp, President of Gazelles International Coaching Association

"*The Curve Ahead* is a handbook for Massachusetts entrepreneurs who want to build successful businesses and fuel our innovation economy."

—Tom Hopcroft, President of Mass Technology Leadership Council

THE CURVE AHEAD

THE CURVE AHEAD

AHEAD

DISCOVERING THE PATH TO UNLIMITED GROWTH

DAVE POWER

palgrave
macmillan

THE CURVE AHEAD
Copyright © Dave Power, 2014
All rights reserved.

First published in 2014 by PALGRAVE MACMILLAN® in the U.S.—a division
of St. Martin's Press LLC, 175 Fifth Avenue, New York, NY 10010.

Where this book is distributed in the UK, Europe and the rest of the world, this
is by Palgrave Macmillan, a division of Macmillan Publishers Limited, registered
in England, company number 785998, of Houndmills, Basingstoke, Hampshire
RG21 6XS.

Palgrave Macmillan is the global academic imprint of the above companies and
has companies and representatives throughout the world.

Palgrave® and Macmillan® are registered trademarks in the United States, the
United Kingdom, Europe and other countries.

ISBN: 978-1-137-27922-4

The Library of Congress has catalogued the hardcover edition as follows:

Power, Dave.
    The curve ahead : discovering the path to unlimited growth / Dave Power.
      pages cm
    ISBN 978-1-137-27922-4 (hardback)
    1. Small business—Growth. 2. Small business—Management. 3. Leadership.
I. Title.
HD62.7.P694   2014
658.4'06—dc23

2013048865

A catalogue record of the book is available from the British Library.

Design by Letra Libre, Inc.

First edition: July 2014

10 9 8 7 6 5 4 3 2 1

Printed in the United States of America.

To Helene,
David, Colin, John,
Cecily, and Patrice

CONTENTS

ACKNOWLEDGMENTS

This book draws on a lifetime of experiences with growth companies, as an executive, investor, and advisor. I want to thank the many CEOs I've worked with, whose boards I've sat on, and whose teams I've led through countless discussions on strategy, alignment, and execution. Among these are Ed Boyajian, Albert Busch, Alex Campbell, Paul Chisholm, Giovanni Colella, Tom Cook, Art Coviello, Dekkers Davidson, Andre Durand, Asad Durrani, Tom Ferry, Mitch Harper, John Hearne, Omar Hussain, Dave Laurello, Doug Levin, Eddie Machaalani, Ken Manning, Scott McNealy, David Patrick, Jack Philbin, Markus Rex, Kyle Rolfing, Eric Schmidt, Mike Stankey, Chuck Stuckey, and Tim Yeaton. I also want to thank several investors and fellow board members who gave me a different perspective on growth company challenges, including Geraldine Alias, Raj Atluru, Larry Bohn, Aneel Bhusri, Simon Clark, Ted Dintersmith, Vinod Khosla, Lisa Lambert, Ray Lane, and David Orfao.

Many colleagues made valuable contributions to an early draft of the manuscript, including Joe Abely, Larry Bohn, Ed Gaudet, Meg O'Leary, Beth Monaghan, Dennis Wiggins, and my colleagues at Gazelles International: Keith Cupp, Hazel Jackson, Cheryl Beth Kuchler, Michelle LaVallee, Juan Carlos López, Cléo Maheux, Daniel Marcos, and Les Rubenovitch. Mark Goulston lent his unique perspective on how to listen to customers. Jane Healey provided valuable research support. Dave Kerpen and Kirsten Sandberg were early champions of the original book concept.

A number of mentors shaped my thinking about growth strategy including Carl Sloane, the late Peter Temple, Paul Buddenhagen, Paul Fulchino,

Mike Lovdal, Frank Mensor, and Chris Meyer of Temple, Barker & Sloane; and Joe Lassiter of the Harvard Business School. Michael Ray and Rochelle Myers introduced me to *Creativity in Business* in the pilot of their Stanford Business School course. Stan Davis educated me on the S-Curve and a different way to think about the future. Margaret Andrews invited me to create executive programs on growth strategy, innovation, and design thinking for the Harvard Extension School.

This book is in some ways a mash-up of some of the most practical concepts behind successful growth strategy. These concepts have survived the hard metal of the market and become valuable tools in my consulting and executive education. My objective in *The Curve Ahead* was to give operating executives some context—when in the life of a real growth company do you use each of these tools, and how do you put them to work? In borrowing many of these tools, I've stood on the shoulders of growth strategy giants including Steve Blank, Clay Christenson, Geoffrey Moore, Verne Harnish, Dave and Tom Kelley, Alexander Osterwalder, Eric Ries, and Ted Levitt.

A special thanks to Celeste Fine of Sterling Lord Literistic and Laurie Harting of Palgrave Macmillan, who immediately embraced the proposal for this book and patiently guided a new author through the publishing process.

INTRODUCTION

This book tackles two important questions:

Why do growth companies stop growing?
How can their leaders sustain growth over time?

There's a great deal riding on the answers to these questions. Growth companies are middle market companies, typically with $10-$200 million in revenue and annual growth targets of 20 percent or more per year. They are the engines of growth and wealth creation in most economies. Investors, leaders, employees, service providers, and policy makers all have a stake in the success of these mid-sized private companies. Unfortunately, most growth companies fall behind the curve before they reach their full potential. Few have discovered the path to sustained, if not unlimited, growth: a proactive approach to extending the life of the current business and uncovering new sources of growth.

Growth companies are different. Their critical challenge is to transition from entrepreneurial focus to a repeatable process for innovation and long-term growth. Unlike startups, they need to make a profit *and* keep growing. But unlike public companies they are still fragile businesses in turbulent new markets. These middle market companies face a unique but predictable set of challenges. Strategies that work for startups or for Global 2000 companies may not apply to them. Growth companies need better tools to monitor the health of their core businesses, a process for building innovation into the rhythm of their business activities, and leadership committed to a culture of innovation—all themes of *The Curve Ahead*.

Growth companies can get stuck. They need to find new ways to keep growing: creating new products and services, developing new markets, scaling operations, developing talent, and attracting the right investors. But too many of these high-potential companies top out before they reach $30 million in revenue (Figure I.1). They become victims of early maturity—the dreaded *S-Curve*—as diminishing returns in many forms erode the original business model. Some become lifestyle companies for the founders. Many are sold prematurely as management and investors decide to throw in the towel. Consider the fact that 50 to 70 percent of software companies are sold before they reach $30 million in revenues.[1] How many of these companies might still be growing if they knew how to find the *next* S-Curve?

When it comes to the health of an economy, the stakes are high—and the opportunity is palpable. Although data on growth companies is incomplete, the picture is clear: growth companies create the vast majority of new jobs across multiple sectors, on many continents. Consider the following:

- According to a comprehensive study by GE Capital and Ohio State University's Fisher College of Business, the middle market is the

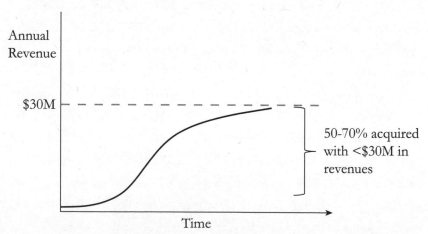

Figure I.1: The $30 Million Ceiling. Source: Aeris Partners, Shea & Company.

largest source of sustainable economic growth and job creation in
the United States today, accounting for one third of total private
employment. There are 200,000 companies with revenues between
$10 million and $1 billion; 80 percent of these companies have
revenues *below $50 million.* If looked at as an individual market
segment, the middle market would be the world's fifth largest global
economy.[2]

- In Europe, the mid-market of the EU-4 (Germany, United
Kingdom, France, Italy) represents less than 2 percent of all
companies but accounts for 29 percent of all jobs and 33 percent of
GDP.[3]

- In the emerging markets of Asia, Latin America, Africa, and the
Middle East, small and medium enterprises (SMEs) account for most
of all businesses, more than 70 percent of the workforce, and 40–50
percent of GDP.[4]

- According to the Kaufman Foundation, 5 percent of US companies,
or about 273,000 firms, create two-thirds of new jobs in any given
year. The top 1 percent, or about 55,000 companies with fewer than
250 employees, generates 40 percent of new jobs in any given year.[5]

- The fastest growing companies are often called *gazelles*—a term
created by David Birch. A *gazelle* is a company whose revenues have
increased 20 percent or more per year for four consecutive years from
a base of at least $1 million. Birch's research indicated that gazelles
represent about 4 percent of US businesses but create 70 percent of
new jobs.[6]

- The Inc. 5000, a list of the fastest growing private companies tracked
by *Inc. Magazine,* demonstrates that growth companies span all
industries and geographies. They also come in different sizes: 47
percent have revenues between $2 million and $10 million, 45 percent
have revenues between $10 million and $100 million, and 8
percent have revenues exceeding $100 million.[7]

A stylized view of the economic impact of gazelles is shown in Figure I.2.
These fast-growing companies, which represent only a sliver of the middle

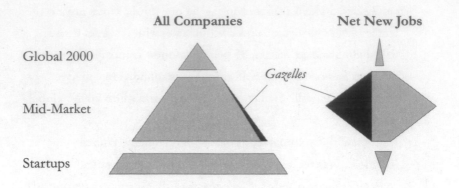

Figure I.2: The Impact of Gazelles on Job Creation.

market, contribute a disproportionate number of new jobs. How can we get more companies to perform like gazelles?

Growth company leaders have few places to turn for practical advice. Most strategy books, executive programs, and consulting services are designed for big company executives. Meanwhile, startups have more free advice than they can use, and much of this advice is not applicable to companies in the turbulent and formative growth stage.

Here is just a sample of the challenges faced by companies that successfully navigated the early growth phase:

- PayPal started life as Confinity, a small company struggling to create a new security solution for PalmPilots. It succeeded as a growth company only because it learned from the market and made a radical shift to become the leader in online payments.
- Meg Whitman joined eBay when the company had $11 million in net revenue. Over the next year she stared down a near-fatal crash in the company's information systems, installed a more scalable business operation, reshaped the growth culture, and led the company through a spectacular IPO.
- The Gap started as a record company that also sold jeans, and not very successfully; Tiffany's had limited success as a stationery

company; Nokia originally sold rubber boots; Nintendo started with trading cards. The list goes on.

For large corporations, Michael Porter's *Competitive Strategy* is essential reading. Startup executives still rely on their dog-eared copies of Geoffrey Moore's *Crossing the Chasm*. I believe that a book on *growth company* strategy is long overdue—how to find the *next* chasm to cross.

I have spent more than 25 years managing, investing in, and advising growth companies—as the CEO of a startup, as a general manager in a fast-growing computer company, as a chief marketing officer in a leading information security company, as an investor in early growth companies, and as an advisor to growth company leaders. Watching dozens of these companies struggle to maintain their early successes has been like watching the movie *Groundhog Day*—CEOs are blindsided by declining revenue growth over and over again. I wrote this book to help growth company leaders, investors, and advisors realize the full potential of these dynamic businesses. Imagine the benefits to employees and shareholders—not to mention the economy—if more companies could successfully run the gauntlet from $10 million in annual revenue to $100 million or more. Today's growth companies can become the successful IPOs, acquirers, employers, and industry leaders that drive tomorrow's economic growth.

The Curve Ahead provides a roadmap for leaders who want to sustain growth over the long term. This roadmap is based on five premises:

1. Every business model matures, following the familiar S-Curve.
2. You can and must *stretch* the S-Curve, but that won't work forever.
3. To sustain growth you need to find the *next* S-Curve.
4. Finding your next S-Curve, with some predictability, requires an innovation process, something every company should have in place.
5. Driving innovation while keeping the core business healthy is the responsibility of leaders.

In addition to providing a fresh approach to innovation and growth strategy, this book is also designed to illustrate *how* growth companies get stuck, and what they need to do to get un-stuck. Each chapter of *The Curve Ahead* begins with the continuing story of a typical growth company called NaviMark. A good story helps us makes sense of a complex situation, and gives us a shared model for how to move forward. In this respect, *The Curve Ahead* is a little like reality TV, showing what it's like to manage a growth company. Although NaviMark is not a real company, it faces the business problems, personal challenges, and strategic dilemmas that are typical of the many growth companies I've known. Don't be surprised if NaviMark sounds like your own company.

I wrote *The Curve Ahead* primarily for leaders of growth companies. But there are many other executives who will benefit from the ideas in this book, including:

- Startup entrepreneurs looking ahead to the challenges of growing their businesses once they've passed $10 million in annual revenue;
- Investors looking to improve the performance of their portfolio companies, and their skills as board members;
- Executives in large public companies responsible for growing new businesses internally;
- Bankers, marketers, lawyers, and other service providers seeking new ways to help their growth company clients;
- Public policy makers and economic development authorities promoting high growth economies;
- Government agencies that want to grow and improve their services (just replace the word "customer" with "citizen").

The book chapters are organized as follows:

- Chapters 1, 2, and 3 outline why growth companies stop growing and what companies can do to keep their core businesses healthy.
- Chapters 4 and 5 explain why companies who want to sustain growth over the long run need to find the next S-Curve. They need a reliable process for discovering new product and service opportunities: *the Innovation Power Tools.*

- Chapters 6, 7, 8, and 9 provide a roadmap for implementing each step of the Power Tools: learn → design → test → model.
- Chapters 10 and 11 define the role of leaders in cultivating new growth initiatives and outline an approach to building innovation into the rhythm of the business.
- Chapter 12 is a summary of the major concepts in the book. Busy executives can use this chapter as a Quick Start Guide.

Steve Jobs liked to say, "The journey is the reward." Growth company veterans know that you need to be ready for a few curves ahead. This book will show you how to navigate them successfully. Readers who want to continue the dialogue will find additional resources at www.powerstrategy.com /the-curve-ahead.html.

ABOUT NAVIMARK

To illustrate the concepts in *The Curve Ahead,* each chapter begins with a brief episode of the continuing saga of NaviMark—a company too caught up in its success to plan for its future. The following brief background on Navi-Mark—its product, leadership team, and financial condition—will prepare readers for the story that begins in chapter 1.

NaviMark is a fast-growing marketing software company based in Boston's Innovation District. Its product, the Navigator, helps marketing executives acquire more customers, promote their products at a lower cost, and make better strategic marketing decisions. NaviMark sells to large consumer products and services companies who sell $1 billion or more over the Internet. These business customers pay a monthly fee to use Navigator, which is delivered as a web application. NaviMark has been featured in the *Wall Street Journal,* named as one of Boston's Top Ten Places to Work, and hounded by investors who don't want to miss the next big thing.

NaviMark's CEO is Meena Kapur, a hard-driving software executive who served as VP of Sales for two successful startups; NaviMark is her first opportunity to run a company. The company was founded by Tim Wiggins, a serial entrepreneur and highly regarded data scientist. Wiggins had done a respectable job as the original CEO of NaviMark; however, the company outgrew his skills as a chief executive. He willingly stepped aside to become Chief Technology Officer when Meena Kapur was recruited to become CEO. Meena's management team is shown in Figure I.3.

The NaviMark board has four directors: Meena Kapur; Tim Wiggins; Jack Huong, an angel investor who led the first round of financing; and Micaela Sanchez, a growth stage investor who led the most recent round of financing.

NaviMark has a revenue goal of $48 million for the current year and has just completed its first quarter. Its historical revenues for the last three years are shown in Figure I.5 along with its forecast for the next three years.

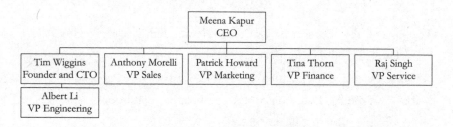

Figure I.3: NaviMark Management Team.

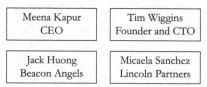

Figure I.4: NaviMark Board of Directors.

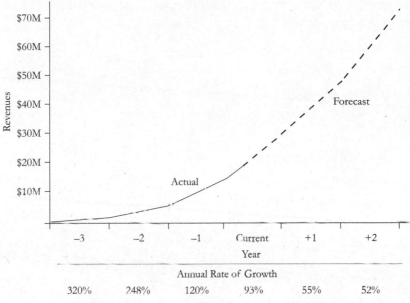

Figure I.5: NaviMark Historical and Projected Revenue.

NaviMark earns 80 percent gross margin on its services business. However, due to heavy investments in Engineering and Sales, the company is not yet profitable.

The story of NaviMark begins in April as Meena Kapur reaches out to Bill Kruse, her former mentor who now works as an advisor to growth company executives.

1

WHY GROWTH COMPANIES STOP GROWING

ENGINE TROUBLE

Bill Kruse woke to the chime of a text message at 6:45 AM.

meet @ flour? need some help

It was six months since Bill had talked with Meena Kapur, a software executive with a string of successes. Meena had a knack for turning up in interesting places and Bill was curious to learn what kind of help she needed.

Flour was a Best-of-Boston gourmet bakery in a historic warehouse with brick walls, high ceilings, and exposed beams. In was located in Boston's Innovation District, close to the site of the Boston Tea Party.

8:30?, *Bill typed back.*

see u there

Bill was an approachable executive known for his strategic problem-solving abilities. Meena worked for Bill ten years earlier running sales at Orion Solutions, a $50 million business services company. Bill sold Orion to Massive Systems, a software industry giant, and then joined a small firm that advised and invested in growth-stage companies.

Bill arrived early for a toasted scone and Flour's "bottomless cup of coffee." Dressed business casual—a blue-checked dress shirt, khakis and brown loafers—he easily blended into the room of local tech professionals. He took advantage of the free WiFi to read the Globe *Sports section on his iPad Mini.*

Meena joined him a few minutes later. A former soccer player at Duke, she was tall and athletic, had long black hair held in place by an exotic looking hair band, and wore her signature bright scarf; she clearly stood out in this room full of business casual.

"Meena, over here," called Bill.

After a few minutes of catching up, and a sports update on the Duke Blue Devils, Bill asked, "So what's happening? The last time we talked I was going to be a reference for you at that MIT startup, Social SecurIT."

"Thanks again for that. Using social networks to improve neighborhood security is an interesting concept. But let's be kind and just say the idea was way ahead of its time. As it turned out, I found a much more interesting opportunity."

"Really! I'm all ears," said Bill.

"Do you remember Tim Wiggins of Digidatum? He founded another company called NaviMark about five years ago. The idea was to build a marketing dashboard—a tool that marketing professionals could use to create campaigns, deliver leads, and manage their budgets. Their product evolved into a big data application that monitors every scrap of information about consumers to make better marketing decisions."

"Sounds like the Holy Grail. Haven't a few companies already broken their picks on that problem?"

"My first reaction as well. But NaviMark became a rocket ship. They landed several consumer marketing companies as design partners and passed $30 million in revenues last year."

"That sounds like a real business. Any investors?"

"Jack Huong invested $1 million in angel financing and became the first board member. Two years later Micaela Sanchez of Lincoln Partners injected a sizeable amount of growth capital to scale the business

and prepare for an IPO. She invested at a high valuation in order to crowd out other interested investors."

"Challenging board member for Tim to manage. Micaela has a reputation for changing CEOs with the seasons."

"For me, actually. A condition of the Lincoln Partners financing was for the company to recruit a new CEO. My name turned up in the search and I took the position three months ago. I'm really excited; this is my chance to take a company public."

"I had no idea. What a great opportunity. So how can I help?"

"Well ..." Meena hesitated. "I'm worried that our revenue growth is starting to slow and I'm not sure why. So much of my time has been focused on customers and investors that I haven't had the time to find the revenue bottleneck."

"I thought you said the business was a rocket ship," said Bill, realizing why Meena was uncharacteristically unsure of herself.

"It was ... until I got there. Then it started getting harder to make the numbers. At the same time expectations are very high; the board wants this company to go public in the next year or so. That means getting the company to at least $70 million in revenues and making sure it can grow at least 25 percent per year for three years after the IPO. I've got six months to get sales back on track and raise a final round of funding."

"No pressure."

"Right. Not to mention the fact that I made a substantial personal investment in the most recent financing."

"Now it's personal."

"Very. I wonder if you'd be willing to take on the role of strategic advisor—to take a look at the business and the team. I could really use a second set of eyes—someone to do a deep dive on the business model. I'm comfortable with a startup, but this business has a few more moving parts than I'm used to."

"No promises, Meena. But sure, I'd be happy to take a look."

"I really appreciate it. I'd like you to start by meeting with Tim and my other direct reports. My assistant Kerry can set things up. I'll also

send you an NDA, some background on the business, and anything else
you need."

Kapur reached for the Galaxy that was buzzing in her pocket. "I'm
so sorry. Can you excuse me, Bill? I've got to take this call."

"No problem, Meena. I'll be in touch."

THE S-CURVE

Every business model matures—it's only a matter of *when* and *how quickly.*
Caught up in the success of their rapidly growing companies, business leaders
often expect growth to continue unabated. They rarely anticipate the speed at
which customer expectations evolve, technology advances, competitors move
in, and the business outgrows the skills of the organization. The net of all of
these changes is a decline in the rate of growth faster than expected. These
leaders soon learn that *sustaining* growth is the next challenge.

In the startup phase, an entrepreneurial team focuses all of its energy
on getting market traction with a new product or service. Success is elusive.
Getting annual revenues to $10 million or more is a heroic achievement that
can take five years or more. Then, like the dog that caught the bus, the fledg-
ling business faces a new challenge—how to make the transition to a growth
company, a *gazelle* that can deliver at least 20 percent in annual growth with
predictability.

After achieving $10 to $20 million in annual revenues, most executive
teams develop aggressive growth plans that look like the graph in Figure 1.1.
Rev the engine, hire more sales reps, ramp up the marketing programs!

Unfortunately, actual revenues follow a different pattern. The company
may continue to grow but at a declining rate. The growth pattern looks like
the well-known S-Curve (Figure 1.2).

We've all seen this curve before. So why does business growth begin to
slow down like this? While the reasons are different for every business there
are some common themes:

- **The original market becomes saturated**. Initially, companies sell
  to customers who are the easiest to reach and most excited about

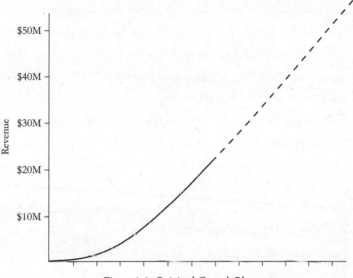

Figure 1.1: Original Growth Plan.

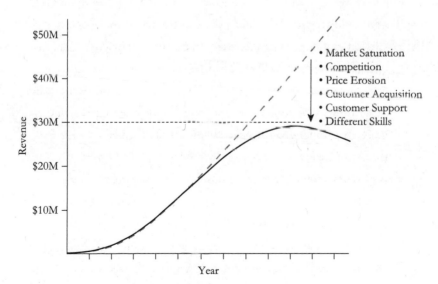

Figure 1.2: Plan vs. Reality: The S-Curve.

the new product; the first mobile phones, for example, were sold to traveling sales professionals who were willing to pay anything to schedule appointments from the road. As a company begins to penetrate its market it needs to work harder and harder, often in new geographies, to find more prospects. Eventually, most of the customers who might want the product now own it. How many more iPods does the world still need?

- **Competitors see the same opportunity and introduce their own products or services**. They *steal* a share of the market, often driving down prices, and make it harder to close new business. After introducing noise-canceling headphones in 1989, Bose had the market to itself for years before competitors began catching up, taking share from the low end of the market.

- **Prices often decline.** The first customers are early adopters who are less price-sensitive; unfortunately, the mainstream customers who drive revenue growth care more about price. The original iPod sold for $399; now you can buy an iPod shuffle for $49. Even if a company's unit sales are increasing, its revenues can lag due to the need to lower prices as it moves into the mainstream market.

- **Customer acquisition gets harder and more expensive**. Scrappy guerilla marketing based on personal contacts and word-of-mouth campaigns gives way to more expensive customer acquisition using advertising, trade shows, and search engine marketing. How much did CareerBuilder have to pay for those great Super Bowl ads with the chimpanzees?

- **A growing customer base demands better support**. Serving a growing customer base—with a great customer experience—requires time and resources. In the early days, product managers and engineers can handle customer support; over time, however, a growth company needs a dedicated support team.

- **The management team that got the team to $10 million in revenue may not have the skills to run a $50 million company**. At one time the entire company could fit in one large room. As the company grows, company leaders need to build and manage larger teams, recruit and develop talent, manage remote offices, build external partnerships, and develop and market multiple products and services. The scale of the business requires more formal processes. Managing this complexity can slow the momentum of the business.

An economist would say that diminishing returns have set in—applying the same effort does not yield the same results.

Realizing that the business has passed the mid-point of its S-Curve can be a painful surprise for an executive team. Companies base their hiring and spending plans on their assumptions about revenue growth. If these revenues do not materialize, the company will have an expense problem. It will have to trim expenses and lay off employees; otherwise the company will need to use precious capital to cover the unexpected losses. This is the kind of surprise that no CEO wants to bring to the board.

LOJACK

There are examples of the S-Curve everywhere we look. Remember the company LoJack, the market leader in anti-theft protection for automobiles?

Founded in 1984, LoJack created the market for stolen vehicle recovery systems. It developed a device that uses radio frequency (RF) signals to track the location of a stolen vehicle. The device is hidden—it can be installed in many different locations in the car. Because police radios also use RF technology, LoJack signals are easy for law enforcement teams to track. LoJack was successful because the product delivered results. An astonishing 90 percent of stolen cars equipped with LoJack have been recovered. These recovered vehicles averaged only $1,000 in damage, in contrast to stolen vehicles without LoJack that averaged $6,000 in damage.[1]

As the company grew it made several adjustments to its business model to support continued growth. In 2001, for example, LoJack changed its distribution model. Until then, LoJack had used its own employees to install the hidden devices. Its new strategy was to turn installation over to the auto dealers who could earn $400 per installation. Over the next few years, LoJack's penetration of the auto market increased from 4 percent to 6 percent.

LoJack also pursued international markets; in 2004, the company acquired a Canadian competitor named Boomerang.[2]

The results were impressive as revenues and margins increased over the next few years (Figure 1.3). In early 2008, LoJack was named one of the Top 200 Small Businesses in the United States by *Forbes* magazine—for the fourth consecutive year.[3] The company's stock price soared from $4 per share in 2002 to $28 per share in 2005. A *Fortune* article in October 2006 suggested that LoJack's stock was a steal: "all signs point to continued double digit revenue and profit growth."[4]

Then things started to change. Market penetration reached a peak at 6 percent of car owners. Car theft rates had declined dramatically, due in part to the effectiveness of the LoJack solution; law enforcement agents were able to break up auto chop shops. As a result, consumers were becoming less concerned about the risk of car theft, and car insurance companies were less motivated to offer insurance discounts to those who purchased the device. There were also new competitors, such as General Motors and its OnStar system that used GPS tracking, the ubiquitous system used in mobile phones, rather than RF signals. Finally, the Great Recession of 2008–2010 drove down the sales of new autos—the number-one driver of LoJack sales. The result was rapid maturity of the LoJack business model and a downturn in revenue (Figure 1.4).

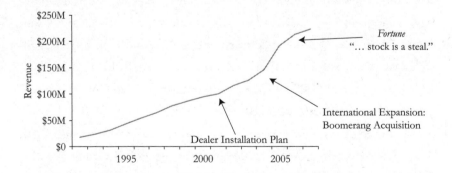

Figure 1.3: LoJack Revenues: 1992–2007. Sources: New York Times *public stock prices data,* New York Times; *and Brian Hindo, "LoJack's Stronger Signal,"* Businessweek, *January 15, 2006, http://www.businessweek.com/ stories/2006–01–15/lojacks-stronger-signal (accessed September 20, 2013).*

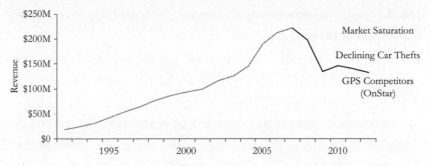

Figure 1.4: LoJack Revenues: 1992–2012. Source: New York
Times *public stock prices data,* New York Times.

This slowdown in growth did not happen overnight. One useful way
to gauge the maturity of a business model is to look at the change in annual
growth rates over time. With the exception of a few years between 2000 and
2005, LoJack's annual growth rate has declined steadily since the 1990s (Figure 1.5).

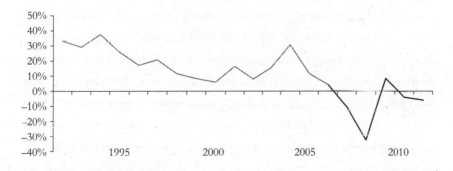

Figure 1.5: LoJack Growth Rates: 1992–2012.

For a public company, a large decline in growth—like the one LoJack
experienced in 2006–2008—can have a devastating effect on company value.
LoJack's stock price dropped from $28 per share in 2005 to less than $4 per
share in 2013. Investors would need to look elsewhere for a growth story.

Could LoJack have avoided this downturn in revenues and value? Perhaps, if the company had laid the groundwork for a *new* source of revenues.
But when the core business of a single-product company matures there are
fewer options remaining for management to drive growth. What was once a

growth company becomes a *value* company as the focus shifts to cost reduction and profit margins.

GROUPON

A more recent example of the S-Curve is Groupon. Groupon defined the *daily deal:* a discount for group purchasing that became an instant success. The early history of the company is a case study in innovation. Andrew Mason founded a company called The Point with the goal of improving online philanthropy for both fundraisers and donors using what he called a *tipping point* model. If someone was raising money to build a new playground, the fundraiser set a tipping point—the minimum needed for the project to go forward. Only when the tipping point was exceeded did Groupon process the credit cards of all donors; this approach removed the risk to donors that their contributions might not go to the intended project.

Unfortunately, The Point was failing miserably as a business and so Mason's backer reportedly gave him six months to find a way to make money. Mason and his team realized they could use The Point's underlying premise as a way to offer group discounts on consumer products and services that created a win-win-win for retailers, consumers, and Mason's company. Groupon was launched and the rest was history . . . at least for a while.

Here's how Groupon and their now-famous daily deals created value. Its sales team would approach a retailer about designing a discounted offer for consumer groups. If Groupon could deliver, say, 20 people who would get their hair styled at a salon, would the salon be willing to offer a 50 percent discount to those people . . . for one day only? For the salon, it was a way to generate awareness and acquire new customers—in place of ads or other local marketing programs. Groupon made money by splitting the proceeds from the one-day offer with the retailer. Groupon's unique asset was the millions of consumers that came to its website daily searching for new deals. Daily deals had become wildly popular with certain consumers, particularly 18- to 34-year-old educated females with disposable income—*an advertiser's gold mine.* The initial response was spectacular and Groupon became one of the fastest growing companies of all time.[5]

In 2010, Google offered to acquire Groupon for $6 billion. Why would Google be willing to pay so much for a two-year-old business? Groupon was serving small business customers—the same customers Google serves—with a complementary, and possibly competitive, product. Google is a marketing services company disguised as an Internet search tool. It makes money by generating leads for small businesses through its AdWords—sponsored links on its Internet search pages. Groupon had the potential to deepen Google's relationship with its small business customers, and help them reach that highly sought after 18–34 female demographic, by delivering both AdWords and Daily Deals to its customer base. You might say that Google viewed daily deals as a new S-Curve, but that's the subject of chapter 4.

Groupon surprised many by turning down the Google offer. Management was riding the tailwinds of an exciting new business model, experiencing growth rates of 100 percent or more per quarter. Groupon decided it could create more shareholder value through an IPO. Indeed the company went public in 2011 at a market value of $16.7 billion after the first day of trading. That was the company's high point.

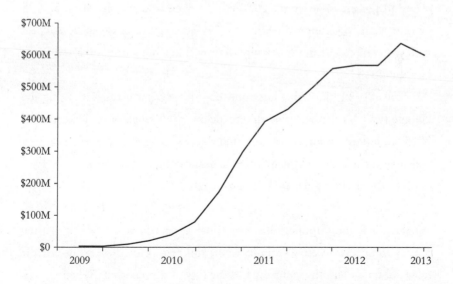

Figure 1.6: Groupon Quarterly Revenues: 2009–2013. Source: Groupon quarterly reports.

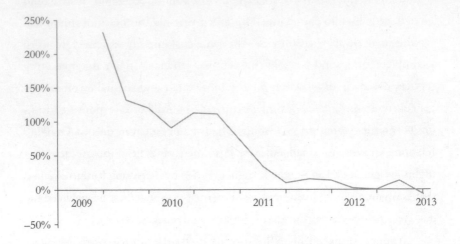

Figure 1.7: Groupon Quarterly Growth Rates: 2009–2013.

Since then, Groupon's growth trajectory has shifted to the tail end of the S-Curve. One cause has been *consumer fatigue*—a term one analyst used to describe the fading allure of daily deals. Another has been competition from Living Social, Google Offers, and other competitors. Still another has been the disillusioned retailers who realized only 25 percent of the value of their offer (50 percent went to the consumer in the form of a discount, and 25 percent went to Groupon) without seeing a return in terms of new repeat customers. In an attempt to reignite its growth engine, Groupon hired a new CEO in 2013.[6]

With 20/20 hindsight, Groupon may have been better off taking the Google deal. Its market value drifted below the Google offer price during 2013. Could Groupon have anticipated the changing attitudes of consumers and retailers? Could management have discovered a complementary service to offset the declining demand for daily deals?

· · · ·

What LoJack and Groupon illustrate is the danger to a business of drifting too far along the S-Curve without a new source of growth. It's not just the financial impact on the company but the loss of momentum. When growth slows, perceptions of the company and its prospects change. For example, it may get harder to hire the best talent; all-star candidates may believe they've missed the company's best years. Similarly, there may be a greater risk of losing your best employees if they believe that career opportunities and financial rewards will be limited in the future.

It can also get harder to fund new growth initiatives. New investors will be reluctant to fund major growth initiatives if they believe the company's glory days are over. Existing investors may become risk averse, willing to fund incremental investments but no longer willing to make big new bets. It's much easier for a CEO to raise $10 million for a new growth initiative when the company is growing at 30 percent or more per year than when the company's annual growth falls below 10 percent. Some investors may wonder whether it's time to sell the company while there's still the semblance of a growth story.

Business maturity in the form of the S-Curve is inevitable for every business model. The growth that came so easily in the early days becomes harder to sustain. Entrepreneurial leaders who have not experienced the S-Curve are surprised to learn how quickly they need to find new ways to continue to grow the business. Experienced growth company leaders understand that you can never know when the business has passed the mid-point of the S-Curve; the most paranoid of these leaders assume that they've already passed the inflection point.

What can companies do to offset the inevitable headwinds of the S-Curve? One option is to *stretch* the curve.

CHAPTER HIGHLIGHTS

- Every business model matures; revenue grows in shape of an S-Curve.
- As revenue growth slows, organizations can lose momentum and value and struggle to reignite growth.
- It's difficult to know where a business is along its S-Curve; leaders are often surprised at how quickly the core business matures.

2

HOW FAR CAN YOU STRETCH?

IN THE TORNADO

Bill admired Meena and her many talents, but every leader has weaknesses. Bill sensed that he would need to move quickly.

He picked up a copy of Inc. Magazine *in South Station before catching the MBTA back to his office in Kendall Square. NaviMark was one of this year's Inc. 5000, the fastest growing private companies in America.*

The next morning Bill received a Dropbox link from Meena that gave him access to the current operating plan, recent board packages, and other company documents. He cleared off his desk to get started. NaviMark had a nice financial story but Bill raised an eyebrow when he saw that the company had made only 90 percent of its sales plan in the first quarter. Given the company's track record this was a warning sign that was easy to miss. Like a pitcher giving up two runs in the first inning, it wasn't a disaster but it didn't build confidence.

He spent the rest of the afternoon preparing for meetings later in the week with the heads of marketing and sales.

THE VP OF MARKETING

Patrick Howard had reserved a table at Sam's at Louis on the Boston Waterfront. Located in Boston's fast-growing Seaport District and offering views of Boston Harbor, Sam's was a favorite of lunching professionals—even on a cool day in April.

"Have a seat, Bill," Patrick called out as the waitress brought Bill to the table. Patrick was a stylish professional with thick-framed glasses, chiseled black hair, and a black silk knit tie. Bill knew that Patrick had a background in marketing communications and eight years of experience as a marketing director at two startups. NaviMark was his first VP of Marketing role.

"Nice to meet you, Patrick. This is an interesting restaurant—if you can find it."

"Thanks. It's one of my waterfront secrets. So . . . Meena tells me you're going to help us with our growth strategy," said Patrick who was anxious to understand Bill's new assignment.

"I hope I can be helpful. But I don't know much about NaviMark yet. I'd love to hear what's happing in the marketing side of the business."

"Sure," said Patrick. "My goal is to build broad awareness of the company and to generate as many leads as possible. I need to help our VP of Sales, Anthony Morelli, meet some pretty aggressive growth targets."

"Makes sense," said Bill. "How are you generating leads?"

"Event sponsorships and social media marketing—these are the best two channels for reaching our audience."

"I see. Who's your target audience?"

"It's every C-level executive who cares about effective marketing—the Chief Marketing Officer, of course, but also the CEO, CFO, and VP of Sales. We want them all to understand the kinds of results we can deliver."

"That's a lot of buying power. How do you measure success?"

"We meet prospects at events and get inquiries on our website. We send all of this information to sales. If the sales team makes its number, we all win. It's as simple as that."

"How strong is your pipeline coverage?"

Patrick cocked his head and gave Bill that puppy look. "Pipeline coverage?"

"I'm sorry. What I meant was the ratio of qualified opportunities in the pipeline to the sales goal. Do you know the overall size of the pipeline?"

"Oh, sure. Our sales team tracks this in Salesforce.com. I can get you password access. I think there's a total of about $25 million in new business opportunities."

"Great. Are all of these opportunities 'qualified'?"

"Absolutely. Anthony's team evaluates each inquiry, and then assigns it a probability. Any deal with more than a 50 percent chance of closing is considered to be qualified."

"And how do you know which marketing programs generate the most qualified opportunities?"

"Hmm. That's hard to track today. But we have an ongoing dialogue with the sales team about which marketing programs they believe are most valuable."

"One more question about your pipeline: how much do you spend to generate new leads?"

"Well, the total marketing budget is about $3 million. Marketing staff expenses amount to two-thirds of the budget. The remaining third is allocated to event sponsorships, public relations, social media, website improvements and the occasional e-mail marketing campaign. The sales team believes that the most valuable things marketing can do are to generate press coverage and secure speaking engagements at big events."

"Okay. Let's order lunch. Then maybe we can switch gears and talk about the product."

"My favorite subject."

Bill needed time to process what he was hearing. He believed that the number-one job of marketing was to deliver enough qualified leads to make sure that the company meets its sales goals. To do this you've got to be good at tracking and measuring everything. Only after you've got a qualified pipeline that's big enough can you think about *brand-building investments such as sponsorships, website design, and media coverage.*

After lunch, Bill walked to NaviMark headquarters on Summer Street for his next meeting. NaviMark was on the third floor of a commercial office building, a few blocks from Flour Bakery. Originally the home of the Howe Leather Company, this nineteenth-century brick building had sweeping views of the Boston Convention Center and the World Trade Center.

THE VP OF SALES

If you asked Central Casting to send you a sales executive, they'd send you Anthony Morelli. Bill felt underdressed when he saw Anthony in a light grey suit, dark blue monogrammed shirt with cuff links, and a modern version of wing tips. Beyond dressing for success, Anthony knew his business. There was no doubt about his ability to close.

"Welcome, Bill. Meena says you can help us grow the business. I'll take all the help I can get."

"Really nice to meet you, Anthony. I hear you and your team are a real sales machine. I'm not sure what I can add but I'd love to hear about how you're managing sales."

"I'll tell you anything you want to know. The way I see it, we've already crossed the chasm and we're now in the tornado. Are you familiar with Geoffrey Moore?"

"Yes I am," said Bill. Moore was a marketing expert with a strong following among growth company executives. He warned a generation of entrepreneurs that early-stage companies need to stay narrowly focused on one or two market segments with a high-touch sales and service approach until they get market traction, or "cross the chasm." However, once the mainstream market for this product emerges—what he called the "tornado"—fast-growing companies need to shift to a dramatically different strategy. To keep up with escalating demand, the company needs to sell a standard version of the product. Think Henry Ford and black Model Ts. All of the effort to customize solutions for different customer

segments goes out the window. The new mantra becomes efficient, high-volume delivery to a red-hot market.

"How do you know you're in the tornado?" asked Bill.

"Experience, I guess, and the fact that the selling process got a lot easier for us. You can never be sure, of course. But we don't believe customers are asking for a lot of customization and training. They're buying our basic product right off the shelf and installing it themselves," said Morelli.

"So how has the sales process changed since you hit the tornado?"

"Two years ago we focused on the commercial market—companies with $500 million to $2 billion in annual sales. We hired consultative sales reps who understood this market. Now we're hiring closers who can open up much bigger accounts. We provide basic training in marketing analytics and then assign them to a territory. We're also planning a major expansion in Europe in the second half of the year."

"Do you have a strong enough pipeline to support your sales targets?"

"So far, so good. The new business seems to keep showing up just in time," said Morelli, smiling with confidence.

"What are you doing to build the pipeline?"

"Our marketing activities seem to attract a lot of interest . . . although I'm not counting on marketing for leads. I expect our reps to do their own prospecting and qualifying. They're experienced sales executives with strong networks of customer contacts."

Bill wanted to go deeper into the sales process. "It looks as though the company came in a little light on its sales targets in Q1. What happened last quarter?"

"I can see you've been doing your homework," said Morelli, cautiously. "We finished last year with a record fourth quarter. However, in doing so we drained our pipeline by accelerating some large deals; these were customers that might have purchased in Q1 of this year but agreed to close in Q4 of last year because we offered them an additional discount. That left us with a limited amount of new business going into the new year. So in Q1 we had to double our efforts both to rebuild the pipeline with new prospects and to close a higher percentage of the deals

that we still had. Overall, we were pleased that we ended up pretty close to the goal."

"I see. That happens to a lot companies at the beginning of the year." Bill could see that Anthony was anxious to get back to business. "How's Q2 coming along?" he asked.

"You sound like Meena. It's coming along OK, but we still have a lot of work to do. As you know, there's always a lot of drama until the last day of any quarter."

"Yes, I'm afraid I've experienced a lot of that drama throughout my career. Before I let you get back to work can we spend a few minutes going through the deals in your pipeline?"

"Sure. No problem," said Morelli.

Bill had Anthony go through the pipeline deal by deal to understand where each prospect came from, and how the sales process was going. After 45 minutes he decided he needed to let Anthony get back to selling. "Thanks, Anthony," said Bill. "And good luck on the quarter."

Bill used the break before his next meeting to think about what Anthony and Patrick had shared. Things were going well at NaviMark primarily because Meena was extremely good at execution—she knew every way to stretch the S-Curve. But her thinking rarely went beyond the operating plan for the current year—this was her blind spot. Bill wondered how she planned to position NaviMark for success over the next two to three years.

Something else was missing. No one was talking about NaviMark's customers—what business issues they were dealing with and how they were using the product. Bill hoped to learn more about these customers from the company's founder, Tim Wiggins.

STRETCHING THE CURVE

No business model can escape the S-Curve. But there are steps a company can take to buy time—sometimes a decade or more of continued growth. Business model maturity is inevitable, but the timing and shape of the existing S-Curve is not fixed.

Stretching the curve should be a priority for any business: it allows the company to maximize the value of its successful products while the market remains strong; it provides the financial stability of a predictable revenue stream; and it generates cash to support future investments in growth. The strategic question is: how long can you stretch the curve? IBM mainframes and Heinz Ketchup have enjoyed a long ride; floppy disks and the Walkman have come and gone.

Among the most common ways to stretch the curve are penetrating current markets, reaching new geographies, serving new market segments, altering the pricing and packaging, and driving consolidation through acquisitions—also known as a *rollup*. Each is worth a brief description.

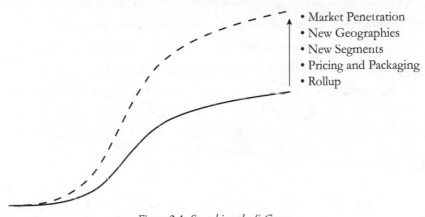

Figure 2.1: Stretching the S-Curve.

MARKET PENETRATION

How much of your available market have you already reached? This is the market penetration question. Before you invest in new products and markets, you want to sell to as many of your target customers as you can. This means, of course, knowing who your target customer is, making sure that they understand your value proposition, and creating efficient sales channels to reach them. There's a great deal of marketing and sales execution involved in penetrating a market.

In any market there is also a limit to the number of *potential* customers who will actually buy a product. Beyond this point, the market is saturated. What percentage of consumers will buy a high-end smartphone such as the iPhone or the Galaxy? How many more Mountain Dew drinkers are out there?

One of the most exciting stories of market penetration comes from an unlikely sector—the food business. The revenue growth of Greek yogurt maker Chobani makes it look more like a software company than a food company. And some have referred to its founder, Hamdi Ulukaya, as the Steve Jobs of yogurt. From a standing start in 2007, Chobani has taken the yogurt market by storm, establishing Greek yogurt as the new standard and generating over $1 billion in revenues in 2012. Not only did Chobani bypass its competitors by increasing its share of the Greek yogurt market to 50 percent, but the company also helped make Greek-style the most popular category of yogurt. Chobani promoted the unique advantages of Greek yogurt: a filling, non-fat snack that is high in protein, and free of gluten and growth

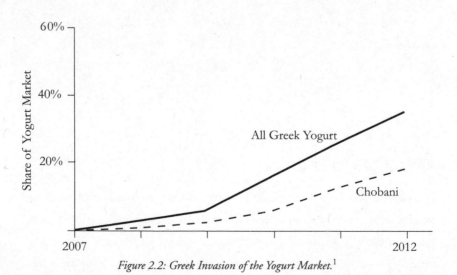

Figure 2.2: Greek Invasion of the Yogurt Market.[1]

hormones. When Chobani introduced its first product in 2007, Greek yogurt represented less than 1 percent of the yogurt market; by 2013, 50 percent of yogurt sales were Greek-style. When your category is taking share from other products, and you're taking market share from your competitors, you can drive a lot of growth.[2]

Chobani has taken a number of steps to penetrate its market. It made a breakthrough in distribution in 2009 through partnerships with super-retailers BJs and Costco. To attract younger consumers it launched "Chobani Champions, the first Greek yogurt made for kids," and became an official sponsor of the 2012 US Olympic team. It also expanded the varieties of its basic yogurt product: more than 24 flavors in 6-ounce cups, 16- and 32-ounce tubs, flip cartons, tubes, and 6-packs.[3]

Where does Chobani go from here? It's charismatic leader, Hamdi Ulu-kaya, has said: "We feel that as long as we stay true to who we are—quality, good-tasting products that are priced fairly and honestly positioned—our growth is limitless."[4]

But there are limits to growth in any market. To continue to grow at 100 percent per year for the next two years, Chobani would have to account for nearly 100 percent of the yogurt market, driving out yogurt heavyweights Danone and Yoplait. Beyond taking over the yogurt market, Chobani would need to convince consumers to make yogurt a bigger part of their diet, substituting Greek yogurt for breakfast foods, snacks, and desserts. The idea is not so far-fetched. According to investment firm UBS: "If Greek yogurt continues its multi-year run, its growth may start to impact other categories such as cereal."[5]

NEW GEOGRAPHIES

Another way to stretch the S-Curve is by finding similar customers in other geographies; you can now find a Subway in Zambia, a Starbucks in Sri Lanka, and a LoJack distributor in Buenos Aires. The first step is to look beyond your home turf.

DataArt, a New York–based IT outsourcing firm, took that first step early on and wound up an Inc. 5000 growth company—for four years in a row. Founded in 1997 by CEO Eugene Goland, DataArt develops custom software solutions for the financial services, health care, and hospitality industries. Goland recognized early on that geographic expansion was critical to success, and opened a DataArt development center in St. Petersburg, Russia, during the company's first year in business. After rebounding from the dot com crash in 1999, DataArt made international expansion the core of its growth strategy; it opened DataArt UK in 2001 to serve the European market with support from several new R&D centers in Eastern Europe. Goland recognized that software programming is a global market, and that virtual development teams can be located anywhere. How well did this strategy work? The company now has over $30.7 million in revenues, 900 employees, and 10 offices worldwide.[6]

The opportunities to serve the global market can be enormous. Do you know what company has more stores around the world than any other? You may be surprised to learn that it's Subway, despite the fact that the company's initial expansion plans were quite modest. When Fred DeLuca started franchising in 1974 he had a goal of 32 stores. Within eight years he had reached 200 stores and needed a new goal. He looked at the density of Subway stores in his best performing areas and realized that he had as many stores in those areas as McDonald's. Since McDonald's at the time had a total of 8,000 stores DeLuca set a conservative goal of 5,000 Subway stores by 1994. By 1990 he already had over 5,000 locations . . . 10,000 by 1995.[7]

Along the way DeLuca maintained a focus on sales growth and profitability of the individual stores. He studied other franchises that had come and gone and concluded that many had lost their focus on the fundamentals of store profitability. DeLuca also engaged his franchisees in discussions about new store locations to avoid cannibalization by having too many stores in an area. Subway's store count passed McDonald's in the United States in 2002, and across the globe in 2010. You won't find a Starbucks or a McDonald's in Reykjavik but you can find several Subway outlets. DeLuca's latest goal is to increase average store profitability by $1,000 per week. It's nice to have an S-Curve that can stretch so far.[8]

However don't let the successes of DataArt and Subway deceive you into thinking that international expansion is easy. Though the product may be the same, the language, value proposition, sales process, distribution channels, and other elements of the business model may be different. Many companies that go overseas for the first time are surprised at the different expectations of customers, the challenge of finding the right partners and sales leaders, and the cost of doing business. Learning what these differences are beforehand can save time, money, and embarrassment—particularly because in many cultures people are too polite to notify you of any cultural gaffes.

AlertDriving, a firm that provides online driver's education courses for corporate fleet drivers, learned the hard way. The company had already expanded into over 20 countries before discovering that its product had some serious cultural flaws. The online dialogue was poorly translated and instructions didn't address subtle geographic differences. For instance, AlertDriving's online program indicated that the center lane is always the safest when driving on a highway, yet in Dubai the center lane is used for passing. It cost the company about $1 million to redesign the product so that it reflected local dialect, driving habits, and cultural nuances.[9]

NEW SEGMENTS

A third way to stretch the S-Curve is to uncover new customer segments. Southwest Airlines, Spanx, and Harley Davidson show the way.

Southwest Airlines broke open a large, underserved market for air travel through its no-frills approach to air travel. At a time when most airline customers were business travelers, Southwest saw an opportunity to fill its planes with leisure travelers. Southwest viewed ground transportation by car and bus as its primary competition. To reach the consumer market the company took a number of steps. It offered cheap fares; the fare for its first flight from Dallas to Houston was $20, comparable to the cost of a bus ticket. It was the first airline to offer off-peak pricing as a way to keep its planes full when there was less demand from business travelers. And it provided convenient access via local airports. To maintain a profitable business model—for more than 40 consecutive years—Southwest has offset its low fares with a strategy of low-cost operations: no meals, quick airport turnaround, no third-party ticketing services, and a standardized fleet of Boeing 737s.

The highly successful shapewear company Spanx was also able to find a new customer segment for its products—going where no shapewear company had gone before. Sara Blakely, a former fax machine saleswoman, founded Spanx in 2002 with $5,000 and an idea for a modern day girdle. It was an idea whose time had come; first-year sales exceeded $4 million, partly because Oprah Winfrey had christened Spanx one of her "Favorite Things." The next year, Spanx generated $10 million in sales.

Focusing solely on women, the market for Spanx shapewear might have reached an early saturation point, but in 2010 it targeted a nontraditional segment: men. When Blakely started getting e-mail requests from men for her body-shaping products, she thought they were joking. Then she enlisted her husband, brother, and father to test some new prototypes before launching the first Spanx products for men: t-shirts that offered Spanx's signature body-shaping benefits. Spanx for Men proved to be a retail hit, selling out in high-end department stores like Neiman Marcus and almost immediately becoming the company's fifth best-selling item on its website, out of hundreds of products. By 2013, Spanx was worth more than $1 billion.[10]

Harley Davidson has gone the other direction. The company hopes to go beyond its mature base of US men over 35 to reach women, the fastest-growing segment but just 10 percent of all riders. "We're not trying to be everything to everyone," said marketing chief Mark-Hans Richer. "We're trying to be our thing to more people." To attract female riders it created a grass roots event called "Garage Party: Not Your Average Night Out," and ad campaigns with the messages, "My time to ride" and "Don't just go along for the ride."[11]

PRICING AND PACKAGING

Another way to stretch the growth curve is to adopt a new approach to pricing and packaging, emulating the successes of Salesforce.com and Skype.

Salesforce.com disrupted the market for customer relationship management (CRM) software by betting on a new way for customers to buy software: software-as-a-service (SaaS). Traditionally, businesses paid a one-time fee to use software indefinitely; this was called the "perpetual-license" pricing model. The customer was responsible for installing and managing the software on its own computer server and database. The customer would also pay 15 percent of the original purchase price annually for ongoing software maintenance and support. If there were a major new release of the software, the company would have to pay an additional upgrade fee, and install the new version of the software.

Marc Benioff, CEO of Salesforce.com, believed there was a better way for customers to buy software that he called "software-as-a-service" or "SaaS." Under this model, the customer would pay a monthly subscription fee to use the software. Salesforce.com would run the software remotely on its own servers. This meant that customers would no longer need to install the software in their data centers or buy more hardware. It also made enterprise software more affordable; instead of making a large capital investment in hardware and software, the customer would pay a more modest monthly fee that required fewer budget approvals. It was like leasing a car. Benioff wondered why anyone would want to own and manage software and launched a campaign called "The End of Software."

His message resonated with IT organizations struggling with tighter budgets and looking for ways to outsource expensive operations. It was also good for business since his company was one of the first software companies with a 100 percent SaaS business model. It was extremely difficult for companies like SAP and Oracle to follow this strategy—shifting from their perpetual license models to offer their CRM software "as a service."[12]

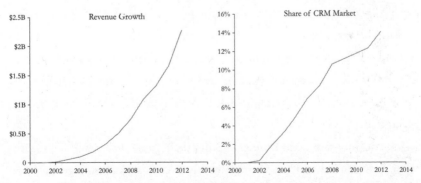

Figure 2.3: Salesforce.com SaaS Disrupts the CRM Market.[13]

Salesforce.com's results speak for themselves. Founded in 1999, the company has grown to more than $2.5 billion in revenue. In 2012, the company became the market leader, surpassing SAP, Oracle, and other CRM software companies.[14]

Skype illustrates another clever approach to pricing and packaging as a way to drive growth. Skype entered the mature long-distance communication industry in 2003 with a different proposition: free voice and video calls over the Internet. Skype discovered a dramatically less expensive way to connect users, relying on the Internet in place of the private networks of telephone companies. Skype has been popular with both consumers and businesses; by 2010 Skype had 663 million registered users, and in 2012 the growth of international phone traffic on Skype exceeded that of all other international carriers combined.[15]

How does Skype make money? It charges users a fee for making Skype calls to landline or mobile phones. This may seem like a modest way to charge for a great service, but these fees add up. Skype was profitable by 2010 with $406 million in revenue.[16] In 2011, Microsoft acquired the company for $8.5 billion in cash.[17]

ROLLUP

One final approach to stretching the S-Curve, particularly applicable to mature markets, is to acquire your competitors. This can be particularly effective in a fragmented industry where small companies compete in niche markets but no market leader has emerged. A rollup strategy can allow a company to drive *inorganic* growth, reduce costs through economies of scale, and establish an industry leadership position. At one time there were more than 130 automobile companies, 2,300 railroads, and 3,200 telephone companies before these industries were consolidated or "rolled up" by the likes of General Motors, Burlington Northern, and AT&T. A modern day success story is Iron Mountain.

Iron Mountain helps businesses store their paper and electronic records securely. Founded in 1951 as the Iron Mountain Atomic Storage Corporation, the company began by storing corporate records in an underground mine in upstate New York. The company grew steadily as regulation required more records storage, printing became cheaper, and many companies found it easier to store their records rather than spending time deciding what to keep and what to destroy. Iron Mountain also developed a predictable revenue model based on a recurring monthly fee for each carton of records stored. In 1995 Iron Mountain was a $104 million private company. The challenge was how to scale the business.

The records and information management services (RIMS) industry is highly fragmented with more than 3,000 companies. Because most cartons of records are moved by truck from businesses to storage facilities, it's a very regional business. Organic growth—from adding new customers or growing revenues from existing customers—has been in the range of 8 to 12 percent per year. To be a gazelle in this industry would require a more aggressive growth strategy—which is what Iron Mountain set out to do.

Its first step was to go public in 1996, using access to public equity to finance a rollup strategy. Iron Mountain then launched what has been called one of the most aggressive growth-by-acquisition strategies in modern corporate history. Between 1996 and 2000, the company acquired 78 RIMS companies, mostly in North America, and then executed a merger-of-equals with a RIMS company the same size as Iron Mountain. With more than $1 billion in revenues, Iron Mountain could declare global leadership of the RIMS industry at the end of 2000.[18]

Having scoured the United States for the best acquisition targets, Iron Mountain focused on acquisitions in Europe and South America through 2003, and then entered the Asia Pacific market in 2005. By 2007 the company had acquired more than 200 companies and grown revenues to more than nearly $3 billion. Since then the pace of acquisition has slowed as the company focused on developing new products and services to drive organic growth.

Figure 2.4 illustrates the impact of acquisitions on the company's growth. Had the company relied solely on organic growth of the business that existed in 1995, Iron Mountain would have ended 2012 with about $390 million in revenues—an average growth rate of 8 percent per year. Instead, Iron Mountain finished 2012 with more than $3 billion in revenues for an average growth rate of more than 22 percent per year.

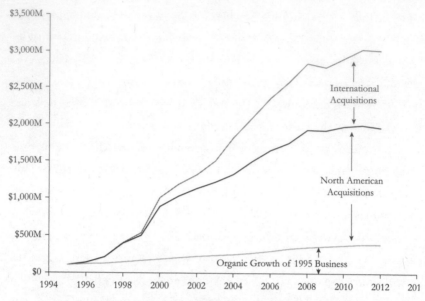

Figure 2.4: Iron Mountain Revenue Growth: 1995–2012.
Source: Iron Mountain Annual Reports, 1995–2012.

How far can Iron Mountain stretch its S-Curve through more rollups? Apparently there's more to this S-Curve as the company made four more acquisitions in the first half of 2013.

Another company that used acquisitions to stretch its S-Curve is Athena-health. Founded in 1997 by Jonathan Bush and Todd Park, Athenahealth created a physician practice management service with an initial focus on obstetrics. As they built their practice Bush and Park were particularly frustrated by how hard it was to collect payments for medical claims. They developed software that not only automated the billing process but was also easy for doctors to use. They then learned that physicians were much more interested in the billing software than Athenahealth's practice management service, and took the advice of one of their early investors: "Get close enough to your customer to understand what they really want. And once you understand what they really want, once that opportunity comes knocking on the door, for crying out loud, answer the door."[19] Bush and Park pivoted in late 1998 to AthenaNet, a SaaS medical billing solution with the easy-to-use interface that doctors loved.

AthenaNet drove the company's growth to $140 million over the next 10 years. Then in 2009, the company began acquiring other cloud-based business information services for health care organizations to extend the life of its franchise.[20] Among these were:

- Anondyne Health, a SaaS specialist in health care revenue cycle data;
- Proxsys, a cloud-based patient communication software company;
- Healthcare Data Services, which provides data analysis for payers and providers;
- Epocrates, a leader in the mobile health applications that has access to over half of all the physicians in the United States.

With the benefit of this rollup strategy Athena Health has passed $400 million in revenue and has been recognized by *Fast Company* and MIT as one of the most innovative companies in the world.

A rollup growth strategy, however, is not for the faint of heart. A number of studies put the failure rate of acquisitions between 50 and 85 percent.[21] A morbid reminder is Loewen Group, a Canadian firm that accumulated 166 funeral homes in the United States and Canada in a bet on the demographics of the baby boomer population. Unfortunately, the firm went bankrupt as there were few economies of scale in funeral home management, demand for funerals never grew as expected, and many sellers sensed that, in its eagerness to expand, Loewen was overpaying for funeral homes.[22]

· · · ·

Most businesses spend the majority of their time stretching the S-Curve of their core business to sustain growth. And why not? It's what the organization knows how to do. It's generally the most predictable way to make the next quarter. But every business needs to ask itself how far it can stretch its current S-Curve, particularly over the next three to five years. Can you expand your available market like Chobani did? Are there unserved geographies in the United States or overseas? Are there high-potential market segments you could target, or changes in pricing and packaging that would open up new growth opportunities? How about a rollup?

If some combination of these options is not enough to meet your long-term growth objectives, you need to search for the next S-Curve. How do you know when it's time to start this search? You never really know because businesses can mature more quickly than expected. You can track changes in historical revenue growth but this is a *trailing-edge* indicator, like looking in the rearview mirror. However, there is an underutilized strategic tool that not only can help extend the life of the current business but can also provide early warning of business maturity—it's the *pipeline* of new business, the subject of chapter 3.

CHAPTER HIGHLIGHTS

- The shape of an S-Curve is not fixed; you can extend the growth of the current business by *stretching* the existing S-Curve
- There are at least five ways to stretch the S-Curve:
  - Penetrate existing markets
  - Enter new geographies
  - Serve new customer segments
  - Change pricing and packaging
  - Acquire similar businesses
- There are limits, however, to how far you can stretch the S-Curve; eventually every business will need a new S-Curve to sustain growth.

3

GET MORE COVERAGE

THE NEXT BIG THING

Bill Kruse had two more meetings at NaviMark. The first was with Tina Thorn, the company's chief financial officer; the second was with the founder and chief technology officer, Tim Wiggins. As he passed the Boston Convention Center on his walk back to the NaviMark offices, he thought more about the company's long-term growth prospects.

THE CFO

Tina Thorn was waiting for Bill in a small conference room, armed with her laptop, a large white binder, and a stack of documents.

"Come in, Bill. Meena's told me a lot about you."

"Only the good things, I hope. I've been looking forward to meeting you to find out how the company is really doing."

"I hope I'm prepared."

"From the looks of things my guess is you're more than prepared. I'm not an auditor. I'm mostly interested in understanding your business model and cash position."

Tina was relieved. Bill was speaking her language. Not one to engage in small talk, she handed Bill a one-page income statement.

"Let's start with the business model. We generate revenue by selling annual subscriptions to our Navigator product. We book 100 percent of the annual fee upfront, but we recognize revenue monthly throughout the life of the contract. Most of our contracts are for one year but Anthony has started to sell some two-year contracts." Tina looked up to see if Bill had any questions. Seeing him nod, she continued.

"We run our software and manage client data in our data center. Our cost of operations runs about 20 percent of revenues, giving us 80 percent gross margins. We then incur operating costs in four areas: marketing, sales, engineering, and administration. Total operating costs run about 83 percent of sales, leaving us a small loss equal to about 3 percent of sales. We could make the business profitable if we wanted to by trimming some of our expenses but right now we're investing in growth."

	Percent of Sales
Sales	100%
Cost of Goods Sold	20%
Gross Margin	80%
Operating Costs	
Marketing	8%
Sales	25%
Engineering	35%
Administration	15%
Total	83%

Figure 3.1: Navimark Business Model.

Tina looked up at Bill, *"Is this what you're looking for? Am I going too fast?"*

"You're right on the money," said Bill, searching for a smile from a very serious CFO. *"Keep going."*

"OK, we have about $6 million in cash, which we watch carefully. We want to protect ourselves in case of a weak quarter. Right now we're

debating whether we should raise another $10 million in private equity to give us a cushion and allow us to invest more."

"Thank you, Tina. That's a very succinct financial picture of the company. It looks as though most of your expenses are in sales and engineering. What's the thinking behind this allocation of resources?"

"Direct sales are what drive our top line. We need to keep hiring and training new sales representatives. These reps need about three quarters of training and experience before they can carry a full quota of $1.5 million. With sales force turnover of about 15 percent we plan to hire two to three new reps per quarter this year. It's a big investment but it's the approach that's gotten us here. As far as the engineering investment goes, Tim is convinced that we need to bet on big data technology—he says it's the next big thing. The ability to sort through massive amounts of customer data could give us a huge advantage; but the tools and infrastructure are not yet mature so we need to custom-build most of our own solution."

"How did you arrive at the marketing budget?"

"We need the company to be visible at certain events and in selected industry publications. Marketing VPs are never satisfied but Patrick seems pretty comfortable with the current budget."

"Meena also told me you have plans to go public in two years. How do you see the company getting there?"

"As you can imagine, our company has become very popular with investment bankers," Tina said with pride. "We've had inquiries from more than two dozen firms over the last six months. They tell us we could take the company public with revenues of $70 to $80 million, and modest profitability of say $5 million. The key is to show predictable growth of at least 30 percent per year."

"According to your forecast, that could be two years from now. Do you believe the company is on track to deliver this kind of growth?"

"I do. I think we have a business model that works, and if we can keep executing we can scale the business to $100 million and beyond. We're in a great market."

Bill paused. "One more thing. It looks as though you came in just under plan last quarter. Is that any cause for concern?"

"Oh, you must be looking at the bookings number. We did make our revenue target for Q1. The nice thing about our SaaS business model is that our subscription pricing gives us very predictable recurring revenue. As long as Anthony can make up the bookings shortfall, we'll stay on our revenue plan," said Tina.

Bill wasn't so sure about all of this. Bookings are an early indicator of the company's future revenue trajectory. You need new bookings today to drive monthly revenue growth over the next year.

"Thank you, Tina."

"Can I show you around the office before your meeting with Tim?"

"Yes, I'd appreciate an office tour."

"I think you'll like Tim. He has an amazing vision for the company," said Tina as they started on their tour.

THE CTO

Tim was the technical visionary behind NaviMark's business intelligence software. With two successful startups behind him, he was what venture capitalists referred to as a backable entrepreneur. Bill wanted to find out what Tim knew about solving marketing problems with data analytics, and what R&D agenda he was planning.

He found Tim in a glass-walled conference room having an animated discussion with four engineers. The white board was full of schematics that were only vaguely recognizable to the layperson. Tim left the meeting to greet Bill.

"You must be Bill," said Tim. "You're just in time. I was about to get cornered by our senior architects. We're mapping out our big data strategy."

"It looks intimidating," said Bill. "All I recognize are the pictures of the clouds."

"Let's head to my desk and I can tell you more."

One look at his office told Bill that there were many sides to Tim. In the corner was a large table with technical gear, drawings, and manuals you might expect in the workshop of an inventor. On the walls were abstract art works in brilliant colors. Tim sat in a Herman Miller chair behind a contemporary desk with a glass top. Somehow it all worked.

"This is a really exciting time for NaviMark," said Tim.

"It seems as though the company has a lot of momentum," Bill replied.

"That's right. We've been at this for more than seven years and I feel like we've finally broken the code. And with the new releases we're planning, things can only get better."

"I was hoping you might give me a sneak preview of what's coming next," said Bill.

"I'd be happy to," said Tim. "The headline is that we're becoming a big data company."

Big data was the buzzword used to describe a new set of technologies designed to make sense of massive amounts of raw data. Every Internet search, security video image, bar code scan, Twitter message, stock price tick, temperature change, and other digital minutia was being captured and stored in digital storage farms that were growing like gypsy moths. The problem for owners of this data was how to recognize important trends that would let them do their jobs better: how to understand what customers want now, tune the manufacturing process, spot the terrorist cell, make the right investment, and so on. The massive volume and complexity of data was making existing analysis tools obsolete. The big data opportunity was to create a next generation of solutions for finding the digital needle in a zillion haystacks.

"Sounds big," said Bill with a little smile. "What's the bet?"

"We believe we can improve marketing decision-making by allowing users to correlate consumer data from a variety of large data stores. Imagine knowing that the customer who's clicking through your website is on vacation, has substantial net worth, is in a rush to furnish a new home, has been checking recommendations on Facebook, and is about *to leave your site because she can't find the item that matches her design. What if you could send her a recommendation or make her an offer before she leaves the site?"*

"Can your next generation product do that?" asked Kruse.

"Not yet," said Tim with a determined look. "The problem is that there's no good infrastructure for extracting, cleaning, and organizing this kind of data. Imagine working with a spreadsheet that has a trillion columns."

"It hurts my head to think about it," said Bill. "Are any infrastructure companies working on this problem?"

"None that are approaching the problem the right way," said Tim. "By the time anything useful is available, we'll have lost our jump on the market."

"OK, let's say you can get this built and into the market quickly. Will customers know what to do with it?"

"We can help them set it up. Besides, we're also building easy-to-use tools for designing custom big data solutions," said Tim with a tone that bordered on what-about-my-big-data-strategy-don't-you-get.

"Have your customers been asking for this?" asked Bill innocently.

"Our customers? That's not where we get our product ideas. Steve Jobs—the greatest product visionary of our time—said that customers don't know what they want. It's our job to show them what's possible."

Bill smiled. "Yes, and Henry Ford said that if he asked customers what they wanted they'd have said faster horses."

"Exactly," said Tim as he folded his arms.

"OK, then what business problem do you hope to solve for customers with your big data release?"

"We know that better data sooner leads to more informed decisions. But each company needs different kinds of data to support the decisions that are critical to their businesses. So we plan to deliver a very flexible architecture that can be customized for each customer."

"When do you hope to ship your big data release?" Bill asked carefully.

"By the way, we call it NaviMark-RT, to support real-time market-ing decisions. Originally we had hoped for a first release in Q4 of this year. But there's a lot we still need to do. So realistically we should be in the market in Q1 of next year—worst case Q2."

"Do you have the resources you need?"

"Yes. We've borrowed eight engineers from the NaviMark product team, and we plan to hire thirteen additional data scientists in Q2 and Q3, if we can find them. Data scientists are the scarcest resources in the big data industry."

"You weren't kidding about this being a big bet for NaviMark," said Bill.

"Yes, but we're sure it's the right bet. And to the risk-takers go the rewards," Tim said with confidence.

Tim gave Bill a demo of an early version of the product. They then talked about the company and the team. Bill knew that Tim was widely admired as a technical leader. He had a track record of success with breakthrough products.

"Tim, thank you for your time and the education," said Bill as it approached 6:00 PM. *"I've learned a great deal about NaviMark today. Congratulations on building such a successful company."*

Bill left NaviMark wondering whether Tim's assessment of the market opportunity and timeline for delivering a next-generation product were realistic. He couldn't help feeling that the company was going to need more time.

THE PIPELINE AND THE S-CURVE

The pipeline is a strategic tool to help senior executives ensure the health of the core business. If the current S-Curve slows too soon, there may not be enough time or resources to develop the next S-Curve.

Every growth company depends on its core business for the bulk of its revenues and for all of its profitability and cash flow. To lay the groundwork for future growth—either by stretching the current S-Curve or investing in a new S-Curve—the core business needs to remain healthy. If the core business sputters, new growth initiatives are often starved for attention and resources. It's a little like the advice the airlines give to adults in the event of emergency—get your own oxygen mask in place before you try to help others.

The stakes are higher as the company increases its expenses in anticipation of higher revenues and starts to make bigger bets on new products and markets. Unfortunately, many growth companies stumble as they outgrow their informal systems for forecasting revenue growth. This is not simply a sales management issue but a strategic management issue that can affect every company function. The consequences of a revenue downturn can be severe: cash shortfall, downsizing to reduce expenses, postponement of strategic projects, and a loss of investor confidence.

To stay ahead of the existing S-Curve, senior management needs to address three questions:

1. How quickly is our core business maturing?
2. Do we have an efficient approach for acquiring new customers?
3. Are we investing enough in customer acquisition?

The company's pipeline or funnel of new customers can help answer these questions. Beyond its role in sales management and lead generation, the pipeline is a strategic forecasting and diagnostic tool that belongs on the dashboard of every senior executive. Unfortunately many executive teams miss the opportunity to leverage this early warning system.

PIPELINE AS BAROMETER

A company's income statement will tell you whether it made its revenue and profitability goals *last* quarter. But the pipeline can tell you a great deal about how the company will do *next* quarter, and beyond. The pipeline should:

- Tell you how much qualified business the company has identified,
- Help predict your chances of making your growth targets,

- Alert you to the need to build a bigger pipeline, change the sales process, or adjust your operating plan.

Perhaps the single most important metric is *pipeline coverage.* Pipeline coverage is the ratio of qualified new business opportunities to the sales goal. For business-to-business (B2B) companies it's the qualified business at the beginning of a quarter divided by the sales goal for that quarter; business-to-consumer companies use a similar approach but over shorter periods. Sticking with the simple B2B example: if the company enters the quarter with $30 million in new business opportunities and its sales goal is $10 million, then the pipeline coverage is "3 times" or 3X. If the company starts the quarter with only $20 million in new opportunities, its pipeline coverage is 2X. Pipeline coverage is like an insurance policy—more coverage at a reasonable price is better.

How much coverage is enough? The answer is different for every business.[1] It depends on a number of factors including how long it takes to close new business—the sales cycle—and how well the company qualifies new opportunities. However, once a company has a pipeline management system in place, pipeline coverage becomes an important barometer of the company's growth engine. If the company generally needs coverage of 3X to achieve its quarterly sales goals but it starts a new quarter with only 2.5X coverage, you can be sure that it's going to be a tough quarter. And if a company's pipeline coverage is on a downward trend from quarter to quarter, it could be a sign of a maturing S-Curve.

However, before you blame the S-Curve, make sure you don't have an issue with your sales process or customer acquisition approach. If your pipeline coverage is strong—3X or more—but you miss a quarter, you may need to improve sales execution. And if you're not investing enough in the right kinds of customer acquisition programs you shouldn't be surprised if your coverage falls short; too often the sales team is the scapegoat for a missed quarter when the real problem was not enough new business.

It takes some work to design a pipeline that can provide this kind of strategic information about the company's growth engine. The next two sections of this chapter provide guidelines on designing and budgeting for such a pipeline system. You may not be responsible for marketing but these sections will help you to participate more actively in the next executive discussion of growth strategy.[2] Those who are well versed in this subject may want to proceed to chapter 4: "Find the Next S-Curve."

PIPELINE DESIGN

A reliable pipeline management system is built from the ground up. It relies on accurate data from your marketing and sales activities. If you're in control of your pipeline then you know your *pipeline coverage,* your *conversion rate,* and your *customer acquisition cost.* You'll also know whether your customer acquisition budget is adequate to achieve your sales goals. It's not difficult if you put the right process in place and start measuring everything.

The pipeline is designed around the sales goal—assume $10 million for the next quarter in a B2B company. It assumes a certain sales *conversion rate*—the percentage of qualified customers that actually makes a purchase. Assuming your business can close one in three qualified prospects, you would need $30 million in qualified opportunities in your pipeline at the beginning of a quarter to achieve $10 million in sales.

The critical term is *qualified.* Without a clear definition of a qualified opportunity, your pipeline can never be a reliable forecasting tool. You run the risk that marketing will assume that it provided enough leads for sales; but if sales misses its quarter it will argue that the leads weren't really *qualified.* Or you might have a situation where a VP of Sales will make too optimistic a forecast based on inputs from sales reps who all use different standards when entering a deal into the pipeline. When it comes to

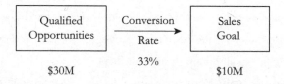

Figure 3.2: The Conversion Rate.

qualification, everyone needs to be on the same page, and that page is the list of qualification criteria.

Think of qualification criteria as a list of questions you could ask a customer in order to learn whether they are your target customer and are ready to buy. For every business these qualification questions will be unique to your customer and your offer. These questions must be crafted and agreed to by both the marketing and sales teams to be sure there is alignment. But in general, there are at least four types of questions:

1. **Problem:** Do you have the kind of problem we solve?
2. **Decision Maker:** Are you the decision maker?
3. **Budget:** Do you have the budget to make this purchase?
4. **Timeframe:** Are you prepared to buy now?

If the answers are yes, yes, yes, and yes, then this is a highly qualified prospect—what some companies would call an "A" lead. The prospect deserves a high degree of attention. Make sure a sales person is assigned and accountable; if yours is a business-to-consumer (B2C) business, don't let the prospect leave your landing page without making an offer.

How do you get the answers to these qualification questions? For B2B markets, many companies use a simple questionnaire or a phone call from a telemarketing rep. Every employee who interacts with a prospect—at trade booths for example—is trained to ask these questions and enter the information into the company's customer relationship management (CRM) system (Salesforce.com, for example). Web marketers qualify visitors by tracking their online behavior: Did the customer download the white paper or engage in an online chat? Why did they abandon the items they put in the shopping cart, as 60 percent of online shoppers do?[3] Designing an effective qualification process is an art; it requires a deep understanding of the customer buying process, ongoing communication across the marketing and sales teams, and frequent tuning. The only way to know if it's working is to continuously track which prospects buy, and then come up with better ways to find more prospects with this profile.

How many raw leads or visitors do you need to yield one qualified opportunity? Once you know this *qualification rate* you can determine how many leads you need at the *top of the funnel*. These leads include all of the names generated through customer acquisition programs such as e-mail marketing, webinars, and Internet advertising. If the qualification rate is 20 percent (that is, one in five leads is a qualified opportunity) and the average sale is $100,000, then the company would need 1,500 leads. Of these, 300 would be qualified leads, 100 would convert to closed business, and the company would make its $10 million sales goal (Figure 3.3).

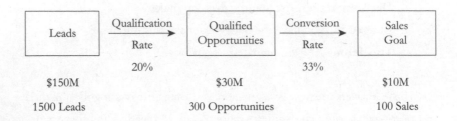

Figure 3.3: The Qualification Rate.

Now, where do you find those 1,500 leads? And how much do you need to spend to get them? The design challenge is to decide what mix of online and offline campaigns will yield the best results. The answer is different for every company but the way to measure the effectiveness of any customer acquisition program is the same—it needs to deliver enough qualified opportunities, at a budgeted cost per qualified opportunity.

When it comes to customer acquisition programs, everyone seems to be an expert. The only way to end the debates is to measure everything. If you're going to spend $100,000 on a trade show booth you need to find out how many qualified opportunities came from that trade show. Here's the marketing accountability imperative: every investment in direct mail, search engine marketing, social media, advertising, or other customer acquisition program must be held to the same standard: *how many qualified opportunities did it yield,* and *what was the cost per qualified opportunity?*

Admittedly, some programs are harder to measure than others. With webinars it's very easy to measure results—you can count the number of prospects who signed up. However, with print advertising it's hard to know who saw the ad and whether it caused them to buy. Some advertisers use a promotional code or a mobile QR code to find out who looked at an ad. Others use surveys to ask their prospects, "How did you hear about us?" Print media has suffered as digital and mobile marketing programs have made it easier to measure the effectiveness of marketing investments. Social media is becoming a more reliable way to acquire customers as marketers learn how to convert community building into new prospects.

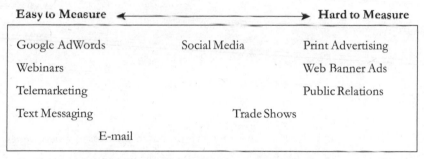

Figure 3.4: Measurability of Customer Acquisition Programs.

One of the most cost-effective, often *free,* approaches to customer acquisition is word-of-mouth or referral marketing. In the early days of Zappos, CEO Tony Hsieh decided to take the budget that would have gone into marketing programs and invest it in world-class customer support. By delivering an incredible customer experience he turned his customers into word-of-mouth advocates for Zappos.

The Internet has spawned a new breed of viral marketing specialists, known as *growth hackers.* These professionals are one part marketer, one part designer, and one part data scientist. Growth hackers like to take the guesswork out of customer acquisition. According to Ryan Holiday, "growth hackers don't see marketing as something one does but rather something that one builds into the design of the product."[4]

PIPELINE INVESTMENT

Once you know what programs work best and what they cost, you can determine the right customer acquisition budget—one that is adequate to meet the company's sales targets. It's simply the number of leads you need times the average cost per lead. In the example above, if the average cost of a lead is $300, the customer acquisition budget should be $450,000.

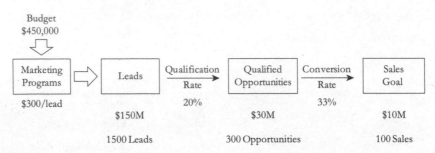

Figure 3.5: The Customer Acquisition Budget.

Another way to look at the lead generation investment is as a percentage of revenues. In the example above, $450,000 would amount to 4.5 percent of sales. Can a growth company afford to spend 4.5 percent of sales on customer acquisition? Before answering that, it's important to look at all of the other costs in a marketing budget:

- salaries (usually at least half of the marketing budget);
- public relations;
- website design and maintenance;
- brand building through event sponsorship or advertising.

The problem for many companies is that their marketing budget is largely committed to expenses *other than* customer acquisition: staff, web design, and brand building, for example. A better way to develop a marketing budget—to be sure that the company is fully funding the customer acquisition programs it needs to support the sales goal—is to *start* with the customer

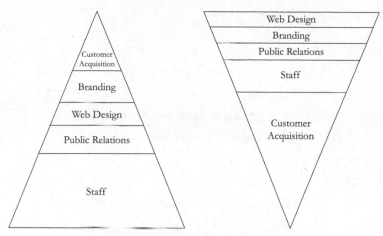

Figure 3.6: Turn the Marketing Budget on Its Head.

acquisition budget. This is a zero-based budgeting approach, also known as *turning the marketing budget on its head* (Figure 3.6). Only after fully funding the customer acquisition budget should a company pay for additional marketing staff or invest in branding building activities.

If the customer acquisition budget is 4.5 percent of sales, then the overall marketing budget, including staffing and brand building activities, is going to be at least 10 percent of sales. That's a pretty affordable marketing budget; many successful growth companies spend 15 to 20 percent of sales or more on marketing. Unfortunately, customer acquisition remains underfunded in too many growth companies because senior management lacks confidence in the productivity of its customer acquisition activities and the predictability of the pipeline.

The pipeline as a barometer of the company's growth engine is only as good as the data that supports it. It can take six months or more of dedicated effort to establish a predictable model. Eventually a company should gain confidence in the pipeline as a gauge of core business maturity, and make better decisions on whether to invest more in customer acquisition, alter the sales model, and adjust its growth expectations.

When a company is doing everything it can to stretch and measure the existing S-Curve it's time to look for the next S-Curve.

CHAPTER HIGHLIGHTS

- The pipeline is a strategic tool to help senior executives ensure the health of the core business. If the current S-Curve slows too soon, there may not be enough time or resources to develop the next S-Curve.
- Pipeline coverage can be a reliable predictor of revenue momentum, but only with a well-designed pipeline and a sound qualification process.
- To ensure adequate pipeline coverage, a company needs to make a big enough investment in measurable customer acquisition programs.
- Turn the marketing budget on its head to make sure customer acquisition programs are fully funded before investing in other marketing activities.

4

FIND THE NEXT S-CURVE

ONE WHEEL OFF THE TRACK

"Can you hear me OK?" asked Meena as she initiated a Skype session with Bill.

"I can hear you and see you just fine, Meena. Where are you?" said Bill.

"I'm in Menlo Park, in my room at the Rosewood Sand Hill. I'm finishing a few days of investor meetings."

"How's it going?"

"Growth equity investors on both coasts really like our story. We should have no trouble raising $10 to $15 million—some want us to raise more. They all just want to make sure that we've got a predictable business model."

"What's your confidence level right now? It seems as though Anthony is feeling a lot of pressure to make up for the small miss in Q1."

"Anthony's always worried about the quarter. That's what makes him a great Sales VP. He thinks Q2 will come down to the last two weeks, as usual. But he seems confident. The deals are there—we just need to close them. In fact I'm interested to hear more about what you've learned."

"Yes of course. I was hoping we could meet in person. Are you flying back tomorrow?"

"No. Not for a few more days. Something else has come up that could be pretty interesting."

"Oh? Tell me more," said Bill.

"Massive has initiated a strategic dialogue," said Meena with pride.

"Really. Who from Massive contacted you?" said Bill.

"Actually their investment banker has asked if I would take a meeting with two executives—one from the big data division, the other from corporate development. He said that our category of software is very strategic to Massive. For every dollar of software revenue we generate they generate five dollars of service revenues."

"Hmm." Bill was skeptical. He had learned the hard way that industry leaders make it their business to know all of the emerging companies in their markets. They have too much at stake to get blindsided by a new solution that might disrupt their market. They also depend on acquisitions as a source of innovation and growth. These companies often put investment bankers on retainer to scour the market for interesting new companies. A call from a banker did not mean that an acquisition offer was imminent; a successful deal would involve a long process of relationship building, due diligence, and internal selling before an acquirer could make a multimillion dollar offer. That said, Bill knew it was difficult for a growth company CEO to resist the excitement of a possible suitor.

"Don't worry, I won't share anything too sensitive," said Meena. "I think it's a good opportunity to develop the relationship. I'll let you know how my meeting goes. But let's get back to the reason for our call. I'm dying to know how your meetings went, what you think of our operations, and whether you see any red flags."

"Alright," said Bill, letting go of his feeling that the Massive discussions could be a colossal distraction for Meena. "I'll qualify all of this by saying that these are just early impressions about your business."

"Yeah, yeah. I've heard you say that before. But I know you've seen dozens of companies like ours, so go ahead and give me the bad news."

"I'll start with the good news," Bill began. "Of course you already know that you're in a huge market with lots of unsolved problems. Your

team is very engaged; I think they smell success. And your numbers tell a great story—outstanding year-over-year growth, strong margins, and what looks to be a path to IPO."

"Looks to be?"

"We'll get to that. First, let me share a few concerns."

"I'm bracing myself," Meena said with a nervous smile.

"Things may look great now, but I'm not convinced you can keep growing at this pace. You've got a great sales leader and the company keeps making bigger and bigger quarters. But Anthony is struggling to make the quarters. Sometimes even a small miss can be an ominous sign," warned Bill. "More to the point, no one seems to understand why your customers are buying, and that worries me."

"What do you mean? Obviously our customers are buying so they can generate more leads with less money," said Meena with a puzzled look.

"I'd like to think so. But your team doesn't really understand how the end-users are working with your product. No one from NaviMark is helping customers configure the dashboard to get the most value out of your product. Furthermore, your sales team has no idea what kinds of results customers are getting. This could be a problem when it comes time for them to renew their annual subscription or buy other products from you."

"So we may have an issue in the future."

"It's hard to tell when this might become an issue. A more immediate problem is that you don't have a reliable way to build your pipeline of new business. You're investing most of your resources in engineering and very little in marketing. I'm used to seeing growth companies spend 15 to 20 percent of revenues on marketing—you're spending 8 percent. And I'd characterize your marketing programs as, well, 'spray and pray.'"

"What do you mean, 'spray and pray'?"

"You don't have a clear idea of who your best prospects are, and what business problems they have that makes them want to learn about your product. You're tossing out a very general message about improving marketing productivity and as a result some, I'll say, random group of *customers is buying the product. Are they early adopters, tire kickers, or mainstream users? No one on your team can say for sure. And I can't find these answers when I look at your pipeline report or talk to your team. The bottom line is, there's no way to know which of your marketing activities is generating qualified prospects. Somehow a bunch of inquiries show up, you hand them to a very hungry sales team and they miraculously close a healthy percentage of these deals."*

"Seems to be working just fine," Meena shot back, though her retreating posture indicated that Bill was on target with his analysis.

"Maybe. But here's the issue: can you scale this model? If you made twice the marketing investment and had twice the number of sales reps, could you double your sales?"

"I guess we'll need to figure that out as we go."

"We'll see. There's another issue. Everyone is so focused on execution; they assume that your current business model has lots of headroom. I'm concerned that you'll hit the tail end of your current S-Curve before you find another source of revenue growth."

"But wait a minute," Meena argued. "Tim must have told you about the RT software project he's driving. That's our next S-Curve!"

"Maybe it is and maybe it isn't. You're a long way from shipping NaviMark-RT, let alone validating the market. I'd hate to bet the growth strategy on that product until we know more."

"What would you suggest?"

"It would be great if we could spend some time with the team mapping out your growth strategy. I don't really understand your new product development process. There are some important ingredients to any innovation process and I'd like to make sure you're covering all of the bases.

Meena paused. "I'm sure you're right about this, Bill. It's definitely something I worry about. But there never seems to be time to map out anything more than an operating plan. I'd like to give all of this more thought." Bill could hear the e-mails piling up in Meena's inbox. "In the meantime, can you tell me the one thing I can do now to support the growth of the current business? I think you would call this stretching out our current S-Curve. You probably think I need to replace my VP of marketing."

"No, I'm not ready to give up on Patrick. However, I do think he could use a strong Director of Marketing Programs—someone with a track record of managing a budget to build a pipeline of qualified leads. I know a few candidates that Patrick might like."

"Sold. I'll discuss this with Patrick and suggest that you guys work together to find the right person. Let's catch up in the next few weeks after I get back."

THE NEXT S-CURVE

Sustaining growth is not about the company's first act—it's about the second and third acts. To sustain growth, a company needs to find the next S-Curve—a new source of revenue growth to offset a slowdown in the core business. It's not easy to do. It means finding a large underserved market and addressing this market with a product or service innovation. Often the business model is very different. But when executed well the company can realize substantial new growth and a head start over potential competitors.

To illustrate the concept of the new S-Curve, this chapter describes several companies that discovered a dramatically new source of revenue growth.

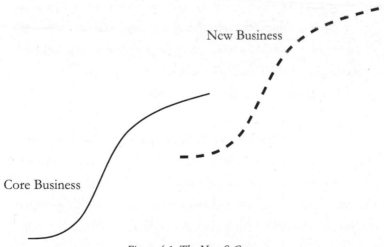

Figure 4.1: The Next S-Curve.

These companies represent a mix of large and small businesses, both high-tech and low-tech, serving both consumer and business markets. Some had the luxury of innovating at their own pace while others needed the next S-Curve to survive. Most grew these new businesses organically while two acquired their new S-Curves. These company examples are organized into four groups:

- Survivors: Cabot Hosiery Mills, Netflix, Southern New Hampshire University
- Small Gazelles: Jawbone, iRobot
- Large Gazelles: Apple, Amazon
- Shoppers: Chegg, EMC

SURVIVORS

Cabot Hosiery Mills, Netflix, and Southern New Hampshire University all saw the writing on the wall. The core business of each was vulnerable to disruptive new competition. Each had to find a new S-Curve to insure its survival.

CABOT HOSIERY MILLS: Cabot Hosiery Mills is a family-owned sock manufacturer based in Northfield, Vermont. Founded in 1978, the company carved out a successful niche providing private label socks to major retailers such as Banana Republic, The Gap, and JC Penney. In 2000, however, low-cost manufacturers from Asia took a large bite out of Cabot's market. By 2003, the company had lost half of its annual revenues and had to cut its staff dramatically. That was when the Cabot family decided they needed a new growth strategy.

Ric Cabot, a third generation owner, led the effort to create a new sock that would reach an underserved market that he knew well—outdoor athletes. Ric, an avid hiker and sports enthusiast, knew from personal experience that hikers, skiers, and runners found it difficult to find a sock that was durable and comfortable. What emerged was the Darn Tough Vermont line of all-weather performance socks. Ric drew on his affinity with the target

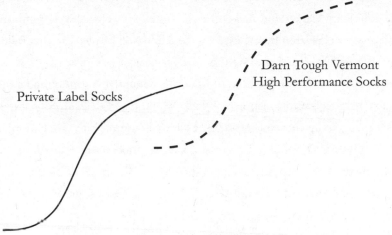

Private Label Socks

Darn Tough Vermont
High Performance Socks

Figure 4.2: Cabot Hosiery Mills.

market and the company's technical know-how to design a completely new sock. He also hired experts in styling and marketing. With this new strategy, company sales quadrupled through 2011. Darn Tough Vermont became a separate brand serving the high-performance sock market while the parent company continued to serve the private label market. In 2012, the company enjoyed the strongest year in its history as sales grew 54 percent.[1] Ric learned a great deal from bringing Cabot back from the brink: "Almost going out of business, if you leverage it properly, is one of the best experiences to emerge from because you see the mistakes, the warning signs a lot sooner," he says. "You try to take a longer-term view of the business—not just what I need to do today, but what will ensure the best tomorrow?"[2]

NETFLIX: Sometimes a company has no option but to race to the next S-Curve. Disruptive products and business models can change the structure of an industry, making existing products and businesses obsolete in just a few years. The movie rental business has been a roller coaster, and Netflix is the latest company to find its original business model eroded by a new video delivery model.

Movie rental started with mom-and-pop retailers—several in every town. Then Hollywood Video created a market-leading franchise, replacing local video stores with a branded professional operation. Soon after, Blockbuster developed a new business model, using information technology to track demand in every market and make sure that its stores were stocked with multiple copies of the latest blockbuster movie. Hollywood Video couldn't follow this strategy fast enough and went out of business.

In 1999, newcomer Netflix introduced a disruptive business model that was more attractive to consumers. Netflix would mail DVDs from its extensive catalog, using a pricing model that allowed customers to watch as many of its movies as they wanted without a late fee. Blockbuster was caught off guard by this new distribution model and went bankrupt. Still, Netflix knew that within a few years it would need to transition to yet another delivery model for movie rental—video streaming.

With video streaming you don't need to wait for your video to come in the mail and you don't need a DVD player. You can download movies to a tablet or a smartphone from your Internet service provider via Amazon or Hulu. Consumers clearly preferred this model and beginning in 2006 the DVD-by-mail business declined 10 percent or more per year.[3]

Netflix had the foresight to launch its own video streaming service in 2007 to ensure its long-term success. To do so it had to implement a very different business model. In the DVD-by-mail business, Netflix could simply buy DVDs and rent them. With a streaming business model, Netflix would need to license movie rights from movie production houses; this meant higher content costs and a less complete movie library. To ensure continued access to high-quality content, Netflix made a game-changing decision: it began producing its *own* content, starting with the successful series *House of Cards.* In doing so, Netflix was *backward integrating* into the production business and competing with Home Box Office (HBO).[4]

The company's new strategy has paid off. In 2012, Netflix generated more than two-thirds of its $3.6 billion in revenues from video streaming, and its market value approached an all-time high. In the first quarter of 2013, Netflix gained 2 million US customers, putting their total number of paid subscribers at 29.2 million.[5] Its original shows, including *House of Cards,* received 14 Emmy nominations. Netflix appears to have navigated the transition to this new S-Curve, but the history of the movie rental business suggests that the company will need to keep its eye out for the next disruption in movie rental.

SOUTHERN NEW HAMPSHIRE UNIVERSITY: The higher education industry is being transformed by online education. Today, online education is a mash-up of free and fee-based course offerings from private businesses and nonprofit institutions. On one end of this spectrum are elite universities like Stanford and Harvard offering free massive open online courses or "MOOCs." On the other end are private companies such as the University of Phoenix, under scrutiny for aggressive marketing and high student loan default rates.[6] And then there is Southern New Hampshire University (SNHU), a small 80-year-old university that punches above its weight in the online education business.

When Paul LeBlanc became president of SNHU ten years ago, it was a quaint red brick campus with fewer than 3,000 students. Its online education program was "a sleepy operation in a nondescript corner of the main campus." Sensing they were missing an opportunity, LeBlanc decided to design a radically different online strategy for the college.[7]

LeBlanc's online education plan for SNHU has been greatly influenced by Harvard Business School professor Clay Christensen, who coined the phrase "disruptive innovation"—defined as the way in which less visible new entrants with "good enough" products and services move up market to displace more established companies. LeBlanc elaborated, "In Christensen's view, higher education, with its skyrocketing costs, is ripe for a revolution; he predicts that in 15 years, half of all universities will be out of business."[8]

SNHU now offers online courses in over 150 graduate and undergraduate specialties. It has over 25,000 students enrolled online and has become one of the fastest growing nonprofit online programs in the United States. Its projected revenue for 2013 was $200 million. Despite its nonprofit status, *Fast Company* magazine named SNHU number 12 on its list of Most Innovative Companies of 2012 for "relentlessly reinventing higher ed, online and off."[9]

LeBlanc knows the online education model is still it its infancy and he continues to think about where to take SNHU's online program next: "We want to be the business model that blows up our current business model. Because if we don't, someone else will."[10]

SMALL GAZELLES

Jawbone and iRobot are fast-growing, middle-market companies that made the search for the S-Curve a part of their organic growth strategy. This allowed both companies to diversify their revenue sources beyond their successful first products.

JAWBONE: In 2007 Jawbone launched its successful first product: a sleek wireless headset for mobile phones. Three years later it introduced a second success: JamBox, a hip, wireless portable speaker. Since then, Jawbone has extended these two S-Curves, selling more than 8 million devices since its inception, by rolling out new headphone and speaker products with its signature aesthetic designs and innovative user interfaces.[11]

Not content to remain a headset and speaker company, Jawbone has laid the groundwork for its next S-Curve by venturing into wearable technology, a market in its infancy but poised for massive growth. In 2011 Jawbone unveiled the UP band, a wristband that works in conjunction with a smartphone and web application to monitor a user's health habits 24 hours a day. It allows users to track exercise habits, eating decisions, and sleep patterns.

While on the surface the UP appeared to be a radical shift from its other product offerings, Jawbone's CEO Hosain Rahman believed that in many ways it was a natural evolution for the company: "It seems like a big departure, but once we start talking about the things it takes to make this whole category work, we get into things like making it tiny, having a long battery life, making it fashionable, making it waterproof, working with smart phones, having a rich, visual experience on your smart phone and making it social. This is all stuff we do anyway."[12]

Jawbone is betting that this third S-Curve that will take the company far into the future. Since the UP first launched, the company has raised over $210 million and acquired Massive Health, a mobile health and lifestyle company, and Body Media, a health-tracking company, to further enhance the capabilities of the UP band. To help the company scale its operations, it hired a new president, Mandy Mount from Microsoft, and added two public company executives to its board of directors: Yahoo CEO Marissa Mayer, and Warner Music COO Rob Weisenthal.[13]

Commenting on the company's recent valuation of $1.5 billion, venture investor Ben Horowitz said: "Jawbone . . . is addressing giant markets and attaching themselves to the fastest-growing trends in mobile and tablet computing. A company's valuation depends on how a company executes its product roadmap, and so far Jawbone is doing a spectacular job."[14]

IROBOT: Founded in 1990, iRobot first introduced its PackBot line of robots for the military to help soldiers with reconnaissance, disposal of land mines, and other dangerous missions. Over its first 12 years, iRobot built a $14 million business for the government market. Then in 2002, the company introduced robots for the home, including the now iconic Roomba, a floor-vacuuming robot. iRobot's consumer products put the company on a growth trajectory that led to a successful IPO in 2005. The company continued to launch new products for the home, including the Verro pool-cleaning robot and the Looj gutter-cleaning robot. By the end of 2012 iRobot had sold more than 8 million home robots worldwide and realized over $436 million in revenue.

iRobot keeps pushing the boundaries of robotics technology to uncover its next S-Curves. To augment revenues from its PackBot and home robots, the company maintains a pipeline of next-generation robotic products that it hopes will transform business and health care communications. One is the Remote Presence Virtual + Independent Telemedicine Assistant (RP-VITA) robot. Built in collaboration with InTouch Health, a leader in health care telemedicine, the RP-VITA is an FDA-approved robot that can connect physicians with patients anywhere in the world. This new robot is large, cream colored, and moves on wheels. The size of a person, the RP-VITA has a flat-screen monitor for a head and a touchscreen interface on its chest to allow doctors to interact with remote patients like never before. Explaining the benefits of the RP-VITA, iRobot CEO Colin Angle said: "It's not whoever's in the building, it's whoever in the world is the most appropriate person or team to treat you when you need it. That's the big idea . . ."[15]

LARGE GAZELLES

Sustaining high rates of growth is easier for middle-market gazelles than it is for Fortune 500 companies. But there are a number of large public companies that are committed to high growth and have demonstrated mastery at creating an ongoing stream of S-Curves. Among these are Apple and Amazon.

APPLE: You know the story of Apple's success. But look again at their growth strategy through the lens of the S-Curve.

When Steve Jobs returned to Apple in 1996, its personal computer business was well past the inflection point of its S-Curve. Industry growth was slowing as most business users and many consumers already owned computers. And with the dominant position of the Windows operating system, Apple had struggled to win more than 15 percent share of the PC market. Jobs knew he would need to find a new market to reignite the growth of the company and establish Apple as the leader.

As we now know, the market Jobs chose was portable music. The transformation of the clunky MP3 player into the elegant iPod gave Apple its second S-Curve. The iPod was not only a remarkable product but it was also an amazing business success. From 2003 to 2007 Apple increased revenues from $4.4 billion to $21 billion, with iPod and iTunes contributing more than *half* of the company's revenues in 2008. Some S-Curve. It's one thing for a $50 million company to grow 48 percent per year for four years, but unheard of for a Fortune 100 company. Apple has been the rare Fortune 100 gazelle.

However, from an S-Curve perspective it's more important to understand what happened next to Apple's music business. Revenue from iPods peaked in 2008 due to market saturation, price reductions, and competition. Many Apple customers had several iPods in different sizes and colors and were unlikely to buy another; things only got worse when Apple shipped an iPhone that could play music. Although revenue from selling music on iTunes continues to grow, the combined revenues from iPods and iTunes grew only 3 percent per year from 2008 to 2012. Jobs knew that Apple would need another S-Curve if Apple were to live up to growth expectations. He ended up finding two more.

Apple introduced the iPhone in 2007 and the iPad in 2009. Both products were wildly successful, together accounting for 75 percent of Apple's revenues in 2012. Apple became the US leader in the consumer technology market—ahead of Samsung, HP, Sony, and Dell. In 2012, investors drove the stock to $705 per share, making Apple the most valuable company in history.[16]

Unfortunately, investors have a habit of asking, "What have you done for me lately?" Starting in late 2012, Apple's stock price drifted to a low of $385 in the first half of 2013. Apple continued its profitable growth in 2013, but not at the rate investors expected. There were, of course, product enhancements like the iPhone 5 but nothing radically new like the rumored Apple wrist-watch phone. Spoiled by the spectacular track record of new S-Curves over the last decade, investors wondered if there was anything really new in the pipeline, or whether the company could continue to innovate without Steve Jobs. As one analyst put it: "During Jobs' second tenure as Apple's CEO . . . Apple had a different idea of innovation. . . . In that definition, Apple would target a huge market and introduce a hardware/content bundle that stimulated a consumer buying panic."[17] All eyes are on Tim Cook and Apple's formidable design team, waiting for Apple to reveal plans for its next S-Curve.

AMAZON: Apple is not the only Fortune 100 company that can grow like a gazelle. Amazon has ridden a series of S-Curves in an equally spectacular growth story that is still unfolding. Amazon's first S-Curve was online retailing, which it launched with its online bookstore. However Amazon has *stretched* this S-Curve well beyond books with a wide range of new products that has made the company the world's largest online retailer. You can now buy an automotive exhaust system, a bottle of Australian Sauvignon Blanc, a kayak, a pair of FRYE boots or almost any other retail product in more than 100 retail store categories.

Amazon also bet that people would read electronic books. It's easy to underestimate what a dramatic change in business model the Kindle was for

an online retailer. Amazon needed to develop proprietary hardware and software, and manufacture a consumer electronics device at low cost. But Amazon jumped ahead of the pack of would-be competitors—Apple, Barnes &
Noble, and Sony—by delivering an e-reading solution that combined ease of
use, the look and feel of a book, accessibility to a wide range of titles, wireless
connectivity, and ease of purchase via Amazon's one-click e-commerce model.
Amazon also had some natural advantages in the marketing of the Kindle:
it already knew the target market of book readers, and it controlled one of
the largest distribution channels for reaching these readers—amazon.com.
Leaving nothing to chance, Amazon also acquired Audible Books in 2008 to
reach the segment of the market that likes to *listen* to books (a great way to
make the best of a long commute). Amazon took things a step further with
Whispersync—a web service that allows you to synchronize your reading of a
book both on a Kindle (when you're sitting) and an audio device (when you're
running)—without ever losing your place.

Not content to take on some of the largest retailers and consumer electronics companies in the world, Amazon has launched a third S-Curve as a

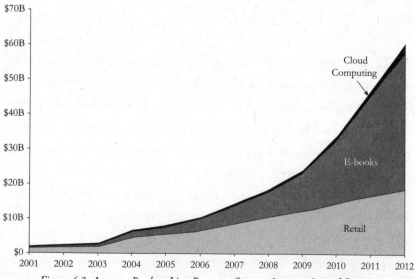

Figure 4.3: Amazon Product Line Revenue. Source: Amazon Annual Reports.

provider of cloud computing services, taking on Google, Hewlett Packard, IBM, and Rackspace.

SHOPPERS

Chegg and EMC acquired new S-Curves, but not by chance. Each company developed a growth strategy to guide its shopping spree. If you know what the next big thing for your customers will be, you might be able to buy it rather than build it.

CHEGG: Chegg built a leadership position in a relatively new market with a questionable future: textbook rental. The challenges were many: low margins, expensive inventory, demand that spikes during the two six-week periods each year when students register for classes, the threat of disruption from eBooks, competition from Apple and Amazon. What were they thinking?[18]

Well before its IPO in 2013, Chegg laid the groundwork for a second kind of business serving its loyal base of satisfied customers: students. Chegg established its customer franchise as one of the first companies to bring textbook rental online; it gained widespread adoption at over 6,400 universities across the country.[19] Delivering an outstanding customer experience, revenue grew from $10 million per year in 2008 to $10 million in the month of January of 2009 alone.[20] But Chegg also knew it was building a different kind of asset: a database of college students that included their courses, opinions, needs, and spending patterns.

With more than 5.8 million registered users in its database, Chegg decided to become a "social education platform" where students can engage up to 365 days a year interacting with study groups, working with tutors, rating courses and professors, and spending some of their considerable discretionary income.[21] Explained Dan Rosensweig, Chegg's CEO: "Facebook is the social graph with the organizing principle around your friends and your social life. LinkedIn is the professional graph, organized around you, your job, your industry, your title and your function. At Chegg, we are building a student graph centered around you, as a student."[22]

Since 2009, the company has acquired a number of companies with complementary services, including: Notehall, a student-to-student marketplace; Cramster, an online study community; Coursework, a service that allows students to rate courses and share them with friends; and Student of Fortune, a tutoring site.[23] Rosensweig elaborated on this approach: "Sometimes you have to slow down in order to grow again. We slowed down, learned the unit economics, and began to build the other parts of the platform . . . that resulted in a high growth company. We now reach nearly 30% of all college students in the U.S., have three robust revenue streams and a diversified customer base—which is powerful."[24]

EMC: EMC Corporation had long known that its core business of storage hardware would mature. In 2002 the company outlined a strategy to transition itself from a one-product success to a diversified Information Lifecycle Management company through an aggressive acquisition program. From 2003 to 2012 EMC spent more than $17 billion to acquire 70 companies. Several key acquisitions gave EMC leadership positions in important growth markets:

- Documentum (content management)
- VMWare (virtualization)
- RSA Security (information security)
- Data Domain, Legato (backup and recovery)
- Greenplum (big data)

EMC's most successful acquisition was VMWare, which it acquired for $625 million in 2004 and whose value has since exceeded $30 billion. VMWare allows software applications to share computers—a critical element of cloud computing.[25] In 2012, VMWare contributed 22 percent of EMC revenues and about half of the company's public market valuation. Acquisition as a growth strategy has a mixed record, but EMC beat the odds with a portfolio approach that delivered at least one home run.

• • • •

These are just a few examples of large and small companies, high-tech and low-tech, that sustained high growth by finding the next S-Curve. Some were proactive, others reactive. Any business that hopes to do the same needs to address a few important questions:

- **How do you make sure the next S-Curve is in place before the current S-Curve runs out of gas?** This is an important question about timing. If your next S-Curve arrives too late, you could end up with a dip or a flat spot in your revenue growth curve. The best answer is to start early. Andy Grove, former CEO of Intel, captured this sentiment in his business bestseller *Only the Paranoid Survive* where he said: "The person who is the star of a previous era is often the last one to adapt to change, the last one to yield to logic of a strategic inflection point and tends to fall harder than most."[26]

- **How many ideas that have the *potential* to be new S-Curves do you need in your innovation toolbox to be sure that at least *one* successful source of new growth will emerge?** The answer, of course, is that you don't know. You need to invest in a *portfolio* of ideas—similar to the way a venture capitalist manages an investment portfolio. How many secret, high-potential projects do you think Apple and Amazon have underway right now?

- **How do you uncover the ideas that might generate a new S-Curve?** This may be the most important question of them all.

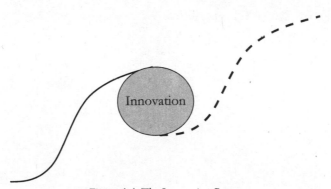

Figure 4.4: The Innovation Process.

To identify new S-Curves with any kind of predictability, the best companies rely on an *innovation process*—which is the focus of the next chapter.

CHAPTER HIGHLIGHTS

- To sustain growth over time a company needs to find the next S-Curve.
- It's difficult for a business to know when it will need the next S-Curve and how long it will take to develop.
- To ensure that a company will have an adequate pipeline of new growth initiatives it needs an innovation process.

5

WHAT'S YOUR INNOVATION PROCESS?

THE BIG MISS

"This is all very exciting, Meena," said Micaela Sanchez as the June meeting of the NaviMark board came to a close. "NaviMark could become one of the hottest companies in the marketing services industry. But a lot hinges on a strong second quarter."

"Mica's right," said Jack Huong. "Any new investor is going to want to see the revenue numbers at the end of June before offering a term sheet for a new round of financing."

"We also need to show steady growth if we're going to have a good IPO story for public market investors next year," said Sanchez. "The bankers will tell you that it's all about predictability."

Meena was feeling the heat. With three weeks to go before the end of the quarter the company had achieved only 42 percent of its bookings goal. "I understand. We have quite a few large deals in our sales pipeline, but this quarter is much more back-end loaded than we've seen before. I'm dedicating the rest of the month to helping Anthony close our biggest deals so we can bring the quarter in on plan."

"I think that makes sense, Meena," said Jack.

The room was quiet.

"As far as Massive goes, I'm not going to take any more meetings for a while," said Meena.

"The more scarce you become, the more interested they'll be when you're ready to talk with them again . . . as long as you keep making your numbers," said Jack.

"Thank you for all your suggestions. I'll let you know how things are progressing over the next few weeks."

"Please let us know if there's anything we can do to help, Meena," said Micaela in a professional tone as she turned to leave the boardroom.

Following the meeting, Meena met with Anthony Morelli to develop a plan for closing the high-potential deals that were still stuck in the pipeline. She planned to visit prospects in New York, Chicago, and San Francisco. Anthony would visit Atlanta, Dallas, and Los Angeles. By reaching out to C-level executives they hoped they could overcome any remaining objections.

Then she called Bill Kruse.

"Hi Bill, sorry I've been such a ghost."

"No problem, Meena. I know you've got a lot on your plate. How's everything going?"

"I've made a lot of progress on our Series C round and raising the visibility of the company with bankers. Discussions with Massive have slowed but they still seem very interested in acquiring NaviMark. My biggest issue now is that our sales productivity has plummeted for reasons I can't explain. I was sure we had enough in the pipeline at the beginning of the quarter but for some reason customers are taking longer to commit. I'm going to spend time in the field to see if I can help close the quarter and perhaps learn more about what's changed."

"I was worried about that," said Bill. "I could never get comfortable with your qualification process. I don't have any answers for you now but I hope to have a better understanding of your pipeline system next month."

"That's not going to help me with Q2," said Meena.

"No. But you need to be better prepared for Q3 and Q4. Do you remember my suggestion about a Marketing Programs Director?"

"Yes. I discussed this with Patrick and approved a new hire."

"Well, I introduced Patrick to someone who we think will be perfect. She has a track record of success in lead generation and pipeline management. She's also got a systems management background and she's maniacal about measuring everything."

"I like her already," said Meena. "What's her name? I think Patrick may have mentioned something about her."

"Her name is Kemi Ramu and she starts this week," said Bill. "She'll be going through the pipeline, your win-loss record, and the effectiveness of your marketing programs. I'll warn you now—she's going to make a strong case to spend more on customer acquisition programs."

"I'm open-minded. I just need to overcome my fear that too many marketing dollars disappear in the mysterious black hole of lead generation."

"Wait. I thought NaviMark was in the business of solving that problem for your customers. It sounds like the shoemaker's children have no shoes."

"Most of our customers sell to consumer markets," Meena backpedaled.

"I think we should schedule a working session with Kemi after you close the quarter. There's a lot to discuss about the ways NaviMark can acquire more customers."

"Sounds good," said Meena. "And I know you wanted to schedule an offsite to discuss our growth strategy. Maybe we can get this on the calendar for August."

"I think that could be a very productive session," said Bill.

"Thanks again for all your help. I need to run."

Meena's experiences over the next three weeks were like the twelve labors of Hercules. She learned firsthand why deals weren't closing. It wasn't about good sales techniques. The new customers she talked with weren't ready to buy the NaviMark Navigator. It wasn't a must-have solution to a critical business problem. And the customers who were supposed to buy additional licenses hadn't learned enough about how to use the product.

They didn't understand how they would get a return on their invest-ment. It was a frustrating experience for an executive who was used to winning. With four days left before the end of the quarter she met with Anthony Morelli in NaviMark's New York sales office.

"Anthony, we're not going to make it," said Meena.

"We still have a few big deals that can close in the next few days," said Anthony.

"And we have to try to close every one of them, but that won't be enough. What happened to our sales machine?"

"I don't understand how this happened. We have a very good team and we're following the playbook we created for all of our reps. We're talking to some great accounts, all of whom have enough budget to buy our product."

"They're not ready," said Meena. "They're kicking the tires because they can't ignore any product that promises what we're promising. But we're not ready to deliver on that promise. They don't know how to use the product and they don't see the benefit. That's what I'm hearing. I'm not even sure we're talking with the right customers. If we are, we need to improve our solution to make everything easier for them to get results. How did we get so far off track?"

On July 1, Meena took an early morning walk along Boston Harbor before reaching the NaviMark office. In just a few weeks everything had changed. The company had its first bad quarter, closing only 62 percent of its Q2 bookings goal. It was a disaster with many ripple effects. The fundraising process was now derailed; interested investors would no lon-ger be willing to lead a Series C financing with a company valuation that would meet her board's expectations. She would be lucky to raise money at the price of the Series B financing—a "flat" round. The IPO timeline would need to be reset; bankers would not want to take public a company with this big a miss in its recent history.

Her first call was to Bill. "Hi Bill. Sorry to call so early. Look, we missed big. I'm going to need to change my approach to growing the business. And I'll need to move quickly; my board is going to be asking some tough questions."

"I'm sorry to hear that, Meena," said Bill. "Tell me more about what you're thinking."

"There are some serious consequences to missing Q2 as badly as we did. It goes beyond the Series C financing and the IPO timeline. We're going to have cash flow problems unless we change the business plan for the second half of the year. Our second quarter was not an outlier where we just had some bad breaks at some key accounts. Something more fundamental is happening to our business.

"I'm going to have to re-plan the second half of the year," Meena continued. "We have to take a fresh look at our bookings goals for Q3 and Q4. It's not a question of making up for the bookings we didn't close in Q2; I'm not sure our targets for the second half are realistic. The board is not going to like this."

"I think it's going to be a tough conversation," said Bill.

"I've got to rethink the business model as well, looking not just at pricing but also our go-to-market strategy and our expense structure—everything that goes into the way we make money," Meena continued. "With less cash coming into the business and no Series C financing, we'll have to cut and reallocate our expenses to make sure we can stay profitable while we search for the right growth strategy. I want the senior team involved in these decisions and I'd like your help with that offsite we discussed."

"I'm ready," said Bill.

"However, before we change our business model I want to know more about our customers. I learned a few things this past month while trying to close some of our Q2 deals that surprised me. But it's hard to learn much when you're focused on closing business. Do you have any suggestions for how we can bring more data and maybe some of the customer perspective into our business planning discussions?"

There was a long pause as Meena could sense Bill's wheels were spinning.

"I think the pipeline analysis will tell us a lot, particularly when we include all of the data from Q2. But if you really want to know more about your customers why not have some of your executives schedule some customer visits this month?"

"It's not a bad idea," said Meena. "Our product managers never seem to have enough time to spend in the field these days."

"I'm not talking about your product managers, I'm talking about your executive staff, including you. Maybe create two or three teams, each with someone who is good with customers and someone who understands the product. Mix it up. Have them visit some of your smartest customers from different industry sectors."

"Why would our customers take the meeting?" Meena asked as she thought more about the idea. "We've been selling pretty intensively at many of these accounts,"

"This can't be a sales call. And I wouldn't bring anyone from your sales team. You want to visit with the business leader to exchange ideas. Believe it or not, I think every one of your accounts will be happy to take the meeting, particularly if some combination of you, Tim, Albert, and other senior executives are willing to make the trip. I can coach everyone on how to manage the conversations; if you do it right you'll be doing a lot more note-taking than talking."

"You know, I think this could be just the wake-up call we need. Can you help us get this road show started?"

"I'd love to."

"Thank you, Bill. I need to call my board members now. Wish me luck."

THE INNOVATION PROCESS

Where do gazelles find ideas for new growth opportunities? And how do they translate these ideas into successful new products and services? The best of these companies relies on an *innovation process,* though each company may have its own name and approach for this activity. Unfortunately, most companies lack such a process; for these companies, innovation is serendipitous if not elusive. They have too many unsuccessful product launches, they lack confidence in their new product development process, and they're disappointed with their ability to generate substantial revenues from new products.

Ask each member of an executive team to grab a clean sheet of paper and to map out their innovation process; you're likely to get a different response from every executive. Some will describe a lengthy process that starts with a *market requirements document* (MRD) that is then transformed into a *product requirements document* (PRD) that, in turn, defines what goes into a *product roadmap*. Others will say that their visionary founder is the source of all new product ideas. Still others will stare at the blank sheet.

This chapter explores the fundamentals of the innovation process from two perspectives: the best practices of three companies widely regarded as innovators, and the innovation frameworks of three leading experts on the subject. It becomes clear that there is no single approach to the art of innovation. However, for growth companies there are four important activities that are foundational to any process for developing new solutions. The chapter concludes with a description of the four *Innovation Power Tools*.

COMPANY BEST PRACTICES?

What can we learn from the companies that are frequently cited for their successful innovation processes? Here's a brief look at three of these companies: Nike, Google, and Kayak.

NIKE earned top ranking in the *Fast Company* "Top 50 Innovators" in 2013. From its roots as a sneaker manufacturer, Nike has established itself as a $24 billion athletic shoes and apparel giant; its tag line is "Inspiration and Innovation for Every Athlete in the World." Among its recent innovations are the Fuel Band, an electronic bracelet that measures your physical activity and calorie intake, and the Flyknit Racer, a feather-light, environmentally friendly shoe that Nike says will "turn the shoe industry on its head." To launch one new groundbreaking product in a year is a feat; two is extraordinary. So how do they do it? One ingredient is the Nike Innovation Kitchen, a design center in a secret location to preserve the unique values of its innovation culture (for example: "if you have a body, you're an athlete") and pass these on to future generations of designers. Nike's *swoosh scientists* are trained to be obsessed with "What if . . . ?" questions. The company also integrates the point of view of athletes and consumers through its research and social media channels. Nike doesn't like to share all of its secrets but one interesting tactic it revealed was its decision to outsource a part of the design process for the Fuel Band; it contracted with an industrial design firm to create hundreds of prototypes.[1]

GOOGLE is on everyone's list of innovators, with a long history of successes beyond its search and advertising business including Gmail, Google Maps, Google Docs, Google Books, Google Finance, Google Checkout, and the Android mobile operating system. Recent big bets that are still in their early stages include driverless cars, Google Glass (eyeglasses with built-in video), and Project Loon (a network of balloons providing Internet access to rural areas). Google's founders and chairman are engineers who instinctively created a culture of innovation for its engineering employees. Some of the company's approach to innovation is embedded in the *Google Statement of Philosophy* and its *10 Golden Rules of Innovation:*

- Focus on the end user and all else will follow.
- Attract and retain the best talent through group interviews, a great work environment, and attractive benefits.
- Organize in small, focused teams with three to five members.[2]
- Allow ideas to be shared across the organization through: Google Cafes, a companywide *ideas mailing list,* direct mail to company executives, and internal innovation reviews.[3]
- Encourage engineers to spend 20 percent of their time on new projects that interest them.[4]
- Invest in *big bets* or *long shots.*[5]
- Introduce new products as test or beta products, using feedback from users to perfect these products over time.
- *Eat your own dog food*—that is, make sure employees are learning by working with their own products.[6]

KAYAK remains a leader in travel services through sustained innovation. Its unique culture starts with the hiring process—the company hires only entrepreneurs and, to retain a fresh perspective, there is no indoctrination into a Kayak-way-of-thinking for new employees. Kayak pushes decision-making to junior staff working in small teams, typically with three members; it avoids large meetings or design-by-committee. Designers talk directly to customers to be sure no information is lost. Kayak encourages fast decision-making and risk-taking—a process that it calls *fast iteration*. To gauge the intensity of its innovation efforts, the company tracks how many product or process innovations its teams try each quarter.[7]

· · · ·

These company stories can be a great source of inspiration. But improving your innovation process by borrowing from these *best practices* can be a little like improving your golf game by using tips from monthly golf magazines—they may or may not be appropriate for you and, in any case, you're missing the big picture.

Is there some kind of methodology to innovation? What do the experts say?

INNOVATION THOUGHT LEADERS

Innovation thought leaders offer several frameworks intended for a wide range of innovation challenges in private and public sectors—what some refer to as *wicked problems*.[8] The terminology and the number of steps in each process vary across design firms and academics. But look closely and you'll see that all rest on some common themes.

Tim Brown, CEO of IDEO, describes the three steps to innovation process:[9]

- Inspiration is the problem or opportunity that motivates the search for solutions.
- Ideation is the process of generating, developing, and testing ideas.
- Implementation is the path that leads from the project stage into people's lives.

IDEO believes that the best designs find the sweet spot between human desirability, technical feasibility, and business viability.

Jeanne Leidtke, Darden Business School professor and co-author of *Designing for Growth,* has packaged some of the best innovation tools and practices in a framework that asks four questions:[10]

1. **What Is?** Understand the customer's current situation and the problems they face. Discover their unarticulated needs. Understand what would be the desired customer experience.
2. **What If?** Explore solutions in a world where anything would be possible. This is the idea-generation stage of the process.
3. **What WOWs?** Winnow down a broad array of options to one or two that solve the problem at a reasonable cost with a great customer experience.
4. **What Works?** Use physical prototypes to learn what's feasible and get early feedback from customers.

The Hasso Plattner Institute of Design at Stanford, also known as the d.school, describes a five-step framework for innovation:[11]

1. **Empathize**—Experience the world as the end user experiences it.
2. **Define**—Develop a point of view that frames the problem.
3. **Ideate**—Go beyond obvious solutions and develop new options.
4. **Prototype**—Allow designers to explore and interact with new concepts by creating physical prototypes.
5. **Test**—Test and refine prototypes using feedback from users.

A deeper look at each of these approaches reveals that most experts share a common view of what it takes to solve complex problems across a wide range of domains, from designing a consumer electronic device to improving water quality in developing countries. Each incorporates customer empathy to gain new insights, collaborative teams with diverse backgrounds, the search for unconventional solutions, iterative design and testing, and frequent customer feedback.

What growth companies need is a practical approach to innovation that incorporates all of the right building blocks. It should help growth companies to develop the products and services that can drive the next S-Curve. And it should be a recurring process that connects to the ongoing cycle of business planning and execution. The following four *Innovation Power Tools* provide a good starting point for any growth company.

INNOVATION POWER TOOLS

The Innovation Power Tools, shown in Figure 5.1, include four key innovation activities sequenced as a continuous process. These include: Learn, Design, Test, and Model.

1. **Learn:** If you're not solving a problem for a customer you're not innovating. You might be inventing or creating some interesting new technology. But you are not innovating until you create value by developing a new way for customers to generate new revenue, save time, save money, overcome a major obstacle, or achieve a goal. And so the first step in any innovation process is to understand the customers—their business environment, the issues they face, their aspirations, the deliverables they're on the hook for, and the specific obstacles they need to overcome. This requires listening to

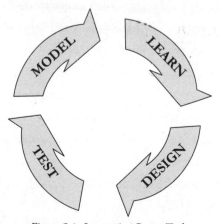

Figure 5.1: Innovation Power Tools.

customers and observing how they operate. The goal is to uncover an unsolved problem or an unarticulated need that represents an opportunity to develop a new offer for your customers . . . before someone else does.

2. **Design:** The customer problem identified in the first step becomes a *design challenge* that drives the creation of new solutions. In most cases there are no existing solutions other than the customer's own do-it-yourself approach. This creates a *greenfield* opportunity—a new uncontested market. However, with any greenfield opportunity comes a lack of structure and an almost unlimited set of options. This kind of problem solving requires a process that is different from traditional business planning. Tools like SWOT (strengths/weaknesses/opportunities/threats) analysis, competitive product matrixes, and market segmentation tend to surface *incremental* improvements to current products in established markets—not the kind of out-of-the-box thinking required to create new solutions. As a result, the most innovative new product teams are borrowing from the toolkits of designers and architects by using *design thinking* to explore a wider range of options.

3. **Test:** Once a team has designed a new solution, it needs to test its concept with prospective customers: Does it solve the problem? Is it easy to use? Are we missing something? Will the customer find the budget to pay for it? It's better to get answers to these questions before the company invests too many resources in product development. Many companies discover product design flaws the hard way—by launching a product that wasn't ready. A better approach is to expose customers to incomplete versions of a new solution, or prototypes, and ask for feedback. But as straightforward as this approach may seem, too many companies bypass this step, generally because they believe it takes too much effort, or because the product teams are uncomfortable exposing partial solutions to customers.

4. **Model:** Once customers have validated a new concept, a company can focus on developing a more scalable and supportable commercial version. The company also needs to decide on a business model: pricing, positioning, customer acquisition and retention, partnerships, and other decisions that are vital to the economic success of a new solution. It's a mistake to assume that the business model for the new solution will be largely the same as the business model for existing products and services. New business model designs—such as *freemium* pricing and direct-to-consumer distribution—can be as disruptive as the new solution itself. Finally, the company needs to view the launch not as the finish line but as the start of a journey of learning from customers and improving the new offer over time. It's just the beginning of another S-Curve!

Unfortunately, many companies take a shortcut to new product development using a two-step process that might be described as *build it and ship it* (Figure 5.2). They skirt past the listening step because they assume that they know enough about what the customer needs to build the right solution. They then want to launch this new solution as quickly as possible, presumably to get a time-to-market advantage; developing prototypes to get interim

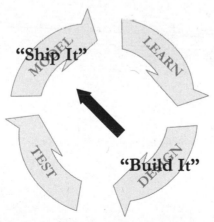

Figure 5.2: Technology in Search of a Market.

feedback from customers seems like a distraction. This approach is often called *technology in search of a market.* There are many well-known examples of products that shipped without a clear understanding of the customer, such as the Segway transporter, the ESPN Mobile phone, and Colgate Dinner Entrees. But a large number of growth companies will readily admit that *build it and ship it* or *technology in search of a market* is a good description of their approach to new product innovation.

How do the Innovation Power Tools fit with the S-Curve? They are the connective tissue between today's business and the next S-Curve. The Power Tools leverage the customer insights and design know-how from the existing business to uncover new ideas that can fuel the next S-Curve. Each of these tools is described in more detail in chapters 6 through 9.

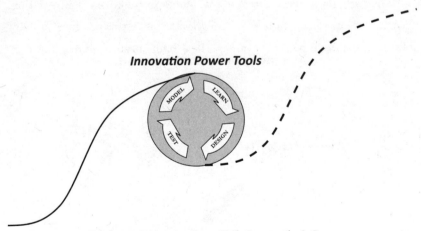

Figure 5.3: Innovation Power Tools Connect the S-Curves.

CHAPTER HIGHLIGHTS

- Few companies have a reliable process to drive innovation.
- Companies that are leaders in innovation, and innovation thought leaders from consulting and academia, have adopted a variety of successful approaches that share a number of core principles.
- For growth companies, there are four Innovation Power Tools that provide a foundation for a repeatable innovation process:
  - Learn
  - Design
  - Test
  - Model

6

CUSTOMER EXPERIENCE IS THE NEW IP

A TALE OF TWO CUSTOMERS

Meena and Raj Singh, NaviMark's VP of Customer Support, arrived in Chicago for a dinner meeting with Benson Moore, Chief Marketing Officer at L'Esprit Cosmetics. Meena had secured a table overlooking the Chicago River at Smith & Wollensky. Chicago had many great steakhouses but this was Benson's favorite.

"Benson, great to see you," said Meena. "Let me introduce you to Raj Singh; he manages our support team."

"Nice to meet you, Raj. I hope my staff isn't driving you crazy. I know we can be pretty demanding."

Meena jumped in: "I always tell the team, what doesn't kill us at L'Esprit makes us stronger." Meena had spent a lot of time with L'Esprit, one of NaviMark's first customers and now one of its largest. L'Esprit was a worldwide market leader in cosmetics. Its multichannel marketing strategy included brick-and-mortar stores, an e-commerce site for Internet shopping, and a mobile commerce site for smartphones and tablets.

"And stronger you are," said Benson. "I think our table is ready."

There were few better dinner venues than the Chicago River on a warm summer night.

"I'm honored that you've come to visit me—we don't have a support issue to solve or a contract renewal to negotiate. You said you wanted to come out just to listen?"

"We've learned so much by having L'Esprit as a customer for our marketing dashboard, we wanted to see if there are other problems we could help you solve."

Benson looked at his watch. "How many days did you plan to stay? This could take some time. You know it's interesting—I mostly get requests like this from startups, and unfortunately I just don't have time to meet with them. But I can't remember the last time one of our marketing services vendors asked me that question. Frankly, it seems like a missed opportunity. We're constantly looking for new ways to fulfill the dreams of the cosmetic customer," said Benson. "Let's turn to my favorite subject—my own problems."

Over dinner, Benson described L'Esprit's sophisticated approach to brand development and customer acquisition across multiple channels on several continents. He described a new virtual reality application for mobile devices that altered photos of the customers to illustrate how L'Esprit cosmetics—different shades of lipstick, eyeliner, mascara, and other products—would change their appearance. The application showed which colors were trending and recommended a collection of products to achieve a certain look. Meena and Raj asked many follow-up questions looking for new angles. As dessert arrived, Benson switched to a new discussion topic.

"Have you done much with repeat buying behavior?" said Benson.

"A little," Raj answered, thinking not much. *"What does that mean for your business?"*

"Like most consumer products companies, we spend a lot of money acquiring customers and then trying to create some kind of loyalty program," said Benson. "But we really don't understand what drives repeat business, or the purchase of new products by existing customers."

"You must have the data," said Raj.

"We have more than enough data," said Benson. "We just don't have the time or resources to do something intelligent with it."

Meena was already brainstorming the possibilities. "Could we come by tomorrow to talk with someone who knows where all this data is?"

"You know your way around our IT group as well as anyone, Meena. Come by at 9:00. I'll send a couple of e-mails tonight to set you up with the right people. If you come up with anything interesting, you'll know where to find me."

Tim Wiggins and Patrick Howard entered a nondescript building in East Los Angeles. It was the headquarters of TSC Electronics, one of the largest contract manufacturing firms in the world, with overseas operations in Chengdu, China, and Wieshaden, Germany. TSC was a new customer prospect for NaviMark. Tim and Patrick had an appointment with Eric Landers, the VP of Marketing, who was completing a proof-of-concept of the NaviMark Navigator. Landers hoped the Navigator could improve marketing operations at TSC.

"Welcome to the parts capital of the world." Landers said as he found Tim and Patrick in the lobby. "We make every kind of widget you can imagine. I just need to find new ways to sell more of them. By the way, I've invited our VP of Operations, Luisa Rivera, to join us. At TSC, we view marketing as a part of an end-to-end business process—finding new market opportunities and delivering low-cost products. Everything we do is integrated and so we want to make sure anything we do with your product ties into all of our systems. By the way, Luisa also runs our IT operation."

"Good morning," said Luisa as they entered a conference room.

After introductions, Landers explained where TSC was in making a decision to purchase the NaviMark Navigator product. "We're still getting up to speed on how to use your product in a business like ours. I'm sure we'll find it to be a valuable business application, but we haven't completed our analysis of how much we'd need to invest in training and implementation, and what return we should expect."

Tim responded. "I know it takes some time to learn to use the product."

"By the way," Rivera added, "we can't seem to get the product to work with Massive's database. Have other customers had that problem?"

"Yes," Tim responded with some frustration. "We've always had a work-around solution but we'll completely resolve this issue in our next release."

Then Patrick Howard jumped in. "We'd be happy to answer any questions about the Navigator but, as I mentioned in my e-mail, we're not here on a sales call. We'd like to learn more about your business and perhaps share some of our thinking about the use of big-data technology to tackle the next generation of marketing problems."

"Big data?" said Landers. "I think our marketing problems are probably more of a little *data challenge. The problem for us is not the volume of data—we don't use social media or do a lot of sophisticated analysis of web-based buying behavior. What we need is a more organized way to capture lots of large and small orders from customers around the world and make sure we deliver products on time. Occasionally we do some outbound campaigns to be proactive about repeat purchases from our traditional customers."*

"Well our Navigator can certainly help you there and I'm sure we can be more helpful in setting it up," said Tim.

"I'm just curious," said Luisa. "Do you have any experience applying your big-data analysis tools to something like robotics operations?"

"That's an interesting problem," Tim said, intrigued by the question. "We do have some engineers with robotics experience. Tell me more about what you're trying to do."

"I'm not sure how much you want to hear about this, so stop me if I go on too long. But our business thrives on our ability to deliver a lot of low-cost products on time. Pardon me, Eric, if I say that marketing is not our biggest challenge at the moment."

"No argument there," said Landers, who took this as a compliment.

"We're using robots in assembly, packaging, and shipping," Rivera continued. "If you're interested I can take you to a nearby building where our robots pick parts for shipping—it's an amazing sight. As you can

imagine, we generate enormous amounts of data across multiple geographies, more than we can sift through. Today our managers have to make all kinds of gut decisions on the fly. But I know we could do better, a lot better, if we had more up-to-the-minute information: for example, are there quality problems with certain batches of finished goods, or production bottlenecks that we could eliminate by reprogramming our robots or changing the process?"

Rivera paused as she thought about the challenge: "Our research team has looked at big-data technology. They decided that the tools are not mature enough to support a business like ours. We'd have to create our own data extraction and integration applications, and then build our own dashboard. Are we missing something?"

"Maybe," said Tim, energized by what he'd heard so far. "I understand the kinds of issues you probably ran into—we've tackled many of them in a next-generation product we call the Navigator-RT. I'd love to hear more about what you're trying to do and see we if we might have some solutions to suggest."

"If you think you can help, I'm happy to tell you more," said Rivera. "Grab some safety goggles and follow me."

Fifteen minutes later, Tim and Patrick found themselves walking through a shop floor with robots moving pallets of inventory and picking parts for shipment. They then entered the Robotic Test Center—a room the size of a tennis court. On one half of the room were 18 robotic assembly machines engaged in different tasks.

"Each of these robots does the work of three people," said Rivera. "Robots are great workers: they can handle 7x24 shifts and they're easy to train. But we need to find better ways to manage these robots; the amount of data they generate can be overwhelming."

Tim could hardly contain his excitement. "We'd be very interested in spending more time with you on this problem. We'd love to see if there are ways we can apply our RT technology to tackle your data management issues."

"When can we get started?" said Rivera.

LEARN

The first of the Innovation Power Tools is learning from the customer. The resulting insights about the unmet or unarticulated needs of customers are what trigger the start of a new cycle of innovation. Without these insights, companies engaging in the development of new products and services are doing more guesswork, and taking on more business risk, than they need to.

Figure 6.1: Power Innovation Tool—Learn.

This observation is based on the important premise that most innovation originates as insights about customers. Not everyone agrees. There's been a long-running debate about the source of innovation: is it customer-driven or product-driven?

THE SOURCE OF INNOVATION

Some argue that innovation is the work of tinkerers, inventors, and creative geniuses who uncover breakthrough product ideas so valuable that they create markets that never existed. In some cases these discoveries are accidental—the 3M Post-It, for example, was the unintended byproduct of a search for a new adhesive. In other cases, inventors are inspired by a discovery that presents a new way to solve an old problem. The Velcro hook-and-fastener technology was developed by a Swiss engineer who was curious about why certain seedpods or burrs would stick to the fur of his dog. Necessity becomes the mother of invention as the determined search for a solution leads to commercial success.

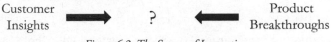

Figure 6.2: The Source of Innovation.

In *The Sources of Innovation,* Eric Von Hippel demonstrated that customers were the primary source of new product ideas for manufacturers. He uncovered the importance of the *lead user,* a sophisticated customer whose need to solve a problem couldn't wait for someone else to solve. Lead users were at work developing their own solutions, and companies that could find and learn from lead users would find a rich source of new problems to solve. Inc. 500 CEOs recently cited *customers* as the most important source of ideas for new products and services (they viewed their own ideas as a backup plan, citing themselves as the *second* most important source of ideas).[1] If you're looking for new sources of revenue, why go any further than the customers you already know?

Does it really matter whether innovation is product driven or customer driven? We might end the debate by declaring that successful product innovation requires a combination of customer insight *and* breakthrough product ideas. But the source of innovation that companies have the most control over is customer insight. Any company that can hire a product visionary should do so—who wouldn't want the next Steve Jobs driving your new product process? But product geniuses are rare, and experimental discoveries are elusive. If you want a predictable process for innovation, the best thing you can do is improve your ability to uncover new customer problems. How many products can you name that were not inspired, at least in part, by a perceived customer need? It's easier to name products that never went anywhere—Google Health or New Coke, for example—because the company was never clear about what problem it was trying to solve.

Many people cite Steve Jobs and Henry Ford, towering innovators, to support the claim that real innovation is driven by product breakthroughs, not customers. Steve Jobs is often quoted as saying, "It's not the customer's job to know what they want," while Henry Ford reportedly said, "If I asked customers what they wanted they'd have said faster horses." The tragedy is that too many managers have used these quotes to justify their decision *not* to conduct research with customers; that's not what Jobs or Ford intended. In fact, both men set out to solve well-known customer problems: MP3 players were too hard to use and cars were too expensive for the average person. The message from Jobs and Ford is not that you should ignore input from customers, but rather that you shouldn't ask customers to design your solution.

LEARN FROM THE CUSTOMER

Where does Dyson get its great product design ideas? In 1974, British industrial designer James Dyson was using his Hoover Junior vacuum cleaner and became frustrated by how weak the suction was and how quickly it clogged up. He was convinced he could build a more efficient vacuum cleaner. It took 15 years and over 5,000 prototypes, but in 1993 he created the Dyson DC01. Within 22 months it became the biggest-selling vacuum cleaner in the United Kingdom. All because James Dyson understood, as a customer, that there was a problem.

Fast forward to the 2013 International Automobile Show in New York City. While many automobile manufacturers were showing off their latest bells and whistles, it was a built-in vacuum cleaner in the Honda Odyssey minivan that stole the show. The idea originated from an engineer at Honda who went on a road trip with his family and was frustrated by all the crumbs and trash that accumulated in his own minivan.[2] Vacuum cleaners may not be the flashiest of products but they don't need to be. Dyson and Honda succeeded because they solved the right problems for their customers.

Amazon's cloud computing business started not with a technical vision but with a customer insight. Most people think of Amazon's customers as the millions of consumers who buy books and other retail products online. But Amazon also serves several hundred thousand *Associates* who sell Amazon products on their websites. To help its Associates increase their sales, Amazon began sharing its development tools, pricing, and product information. In doing so Amazon realized it could help its Associates further by allowing them to tap into Amazon's massive server and data storage infrastructure. The bootstrapped service business that emerged became Amazon Web Services. By listening to its customers, Amazon gained a first-mover advantage, and grew to be the largest provider of cloud computing services—bigger than Google, HP, IBM, or Rackspace.

It's shocking to see the number of companies with good customer franchises that don't spend time with their customers (not including time spent in sales or support situations where attendance is mandatory and the agenda is constrained). Rare are the customer interactions where the only objective is to listen and learn about the problems customers face. Some executives can't seem to find the time; it requires blocking out days on their calendar for customer visits. Others fear that they're somehow inconveniencing their customers. Only 37 percent of Inc. 500 CEOs believe they have a formal process for gathering customer ideas.[3] That means that most companies are missing the opportunity to tap into one of their most valuable assets. The fact is that customers love to talk about their problems. (Really, doesn't everyone?) Solving these problems is the customer's job but the door is open to anyone who believes they can help.

CUSTOMER EXPERIENCE

One important advantage to understanding the customer is to move beyond delivering a better product or service to delivering a better experience. Customers don't care as much about features and functions as they do about three issues:

1. Does it solve the problem?
2. Is using it a positive experience: simple, fast, reliable, and cost effective?
3. Is it easy to get help when you need it?

Ted Levitt, the marketing grand master from Harvard Business School, captured the concept of customer experience best when he introduced marketers to the concept of the *whole product*. It's not just about delivering a product but about delivering a complete solution with an unexpectedly great experience. Levitt argued that for any product there are several layers of customer value. At the core is the *generic* product. A good example would be the original MP3 music player; it was a portable memory stick with headphones and a display, but only a technophile had the patience to make it work. At the next layer is the *expected* product that delivers what that customer was hoping to get. The iPod delivered this by making portable music players easy to use. At the next level is the *augmented* product that delivers benefits beyond what customers expected. Apple delivered this when it created the iTunes store, making it easy to buy songs for a dollar and load them onto simple playlists for their iPod. Finally there is the *potential* product, encompassing additional opportunities to add value to the product, often beyond what customers dreamed about. Who knew we'd be watching videos on these music players, wearing them on our arms while we run, or seeing them merged with smart phones? Levitt challenged every company to create more valuable

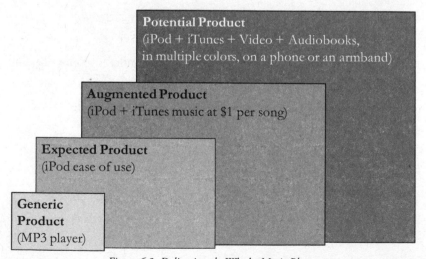

Figure 6.3: Delivering the Whole *Music Player.*

products by using their understanding of the customer experience to create *whole* products.

Here are a few of the companies who always seem to deliver *whole* products and services, and then surprise us with more:

Amazon	GEICO	Starbucks
Apple	Nordstrom	Tesco
Cesna	Rackspace	Virgin Atlantic
Fidelity	Ritz Carlton	Zappos

The best customer experiences seem effortless. Have you returned a pair of Zappos shoes, or rented a Hertz car using its mobile app? If you subscribe to *The Economist* you not only get access to the latest issues on their mobile app, but you can have the articles read to you while driving your Bluetooth-enabled car. These are examples of companies that seem always to be improving the customer experience. Don't underestimate the challenging design work that goes on behind the scenes.

One of my favorite service innovations comes from Tesco's grocery stores in Korea. Recognizing the premium that Korean workers put on saving time, Tesco created a way for commuters to conduct most of their grocery shopping without having to go to a grocery store. Tesco installed backlit billboards that display realistic food aisles . . . in subway stations. Commuters can use their smart phone to order and pay for groceries using their mobile phones.

When you get the customer experience right, you've created competitive differentiation that's hard to copy. A company's customer experience may be more valuable than intellectual property (IP) such as patents and trade secrets. This is why *customer experience is the new IP.*

HOW TO LISTEN

What does it mean to listen to the customer? It depends on the context. If you're interested in customer satisfaction, you can ask, "How are we doing?" If you want feedback on a product roadmap you can give a presentation and ask for comments. But if your agenda is innovation and you're searching for new problems to solve, you need to listen in a different way. You need to stand in the shoes of the customers and imagine how they see the world. You need to learn about their problems from *their* perspective. It's a skill that designers call *customer empathy.*

The way to learn about customers and their needs is to observe them in their daily routines, talk with them in person, listen with empathy and learn about their challenges and goals. You're looking to help them in ways they may not have thought about—their unarticulated needs. You need to sift through a good deal of information to find the pointers for innovation; it's a little like sorting through the human genome—only 2 percent contains the genetic code scientists are looking for.

The best way to have this conversation is to start with open-ended questions and then listen, ask follow-up questions, and take good notes. Mark Goulston, author of *Just Listen,* warns that if you ask people to talk about themselves and their businesses you'd better be prepared to listen sincerely. You need to listen past your *blind spot*—your vested interest in the conversation. To get to *their* there, you need to listen without judgment, memory, or desire.[4]

Getting out to talk with customers may seem like a straightforward approach to uncovering new opportunities, but most executives are uncomfortable with the process: "How do I set up this kind of a meeting? What questions should I ask?" Here's a template to get started:

To ask for the meeting you don't need a detailed agenda or a slide deck. Smart customers understand the importance of customer research. Simply say, "We're spending time thinking about new ways we can help customers like you in the future. Your company has always done a great job of anticipating changes in your market. Would you be available to meet for about an hour to discuss where you see your business headed and the biggest challenges you face?"

Once you get the meeting, start the dialogue with questions such as these:

- What's been happening to the business since we talked last?
- What are your top priorities right now?
- Which competitor do you worry most about?

- How are you tackling the problem of _____?

Then shift to the future and ask what Goulston calls *the impossibility question:*

- Imagine it's three years from now and your business is wildly successful. Look around, what do you see?
- What is something that would be impossible to do, but if you *could* do it, would allow you to realize your goals?
- How could we make this possible?

And a great way to close the meeting is to leave the door open:

- If we uncover some new approaches to tackling one or two of the problems we discussed today, would you be open to a follow-up meeting?

These intelligence-gathering meetings are not just for product managers, though most product managers could be spending more time in the field learning about their customers' businesses *at the coal face.* CEOs of product and service companies have a special ability to access the C-level executives at their major accounts—executives that product managers and sales executives may never reach. This provides a rare opportunity to learn first-hand about the company's future challenges.

Ironically, the more successful your business becomes the greater the risk of losing touch with your customers. Early stage companies depend on customer interactions for their survival. But once they transition to the growth stage, the focus on quarterly sales growth and the scaling of operations drives out the time for more relaxed conversations with customers, the kinds of conversations that can surface new business opportunities or provide an early warning of problems. It only gets worse as companies continue to get bigger. Part of Lou Gerstner's formula for the turnaround of IBM in the 1990s was to require senior IBM executives to spend more time with customers. He sensed that IBM was out of touch with its customers and instructed his top 24 managers, and each of their direct reports, to meet with a least five large and small customers and send Gerstner a report of their visits. This customer manifesto served the dual purpose of helping IBM executives build some customer empathy while also driving a massive fact-finding initiative for Gerstner, who read every report.

There are other ways to listen to the customer besides one-on-one interviews. Social media communities and customer forums provide a way to tune in to a group of customers with shared interests. Vendors are welcome in many of these online discussions as long as they don't promote their products. For companies that need a head start, Communispace can create private, online customer communities allowing their clients to benefit from customer feedback and ideas.

Customer events or customer advisory boards can also provide a forum for customers to describe emerging needs and to provide feedback on current products and services. The best companies understand that feedback is a gift, and they make it as easy as possible for customers to explain what's on their minds.

Before moving on, it's worth calling out a few traps, or shortcuts, that are *not* reliable ways to learn from customers. The first is to use third-party surveys and research reports. These distillations strip out the raw data that can create a deeper understanding of the customer, and lead to the discovery of breakthrough solutions. Relying on a third party robs you of the live interaction, the opportunity to ask a follow-up question, or pick up on an unexpected conversational thread. In many cases research reports are available to several companies in the same industry—the so-called *multiclient report*—diminishing the opportunity for any one company to gain a competitive edge. Research reports are more valuable as a way to *prepare* for field research, to develop hypotheses to test with live customers, or to estimate market size.

The second trap is to use *customer-facing* employees as a proxy for the customer. Some believe that the company's sales and service representatives, for example, understand what customers need because they interact so often with the customer. The problem with this approach is that their interactions are always in the context of a sales or support situation, not an exploration of what else the customer might need.

Nor should you rely too much on your own intuition about the customer, tempting as it may be. Too many companies fall into the trap of thinking, "We know what our customers need, we just need to deliver it." But our understanding is usually too narrowly focused, and limited to the problems we solve with existing products and services, not the adjacent problems that we rarely see. Furthermore, the problems that customers face change over time.

WHAT'S THE PROBLEM?

In the race to make progress, there's a strong temptation to start creating the solution before you've defined the problem. This is the shortcoming of most new product initiatives—few product teams are able to give crisp answers to the two most important questions about any new offer: "Who is the customer?" and "What problem are we solving?"

Understanding the customer and the problem—what Clay Christensen calls the job-to-be-done[5]—not only improves the likelihood of building a product the customer will buy, but it also leads to a better search for new solutions. Back to home video rental for a simple example: any competitor in the 1990s who was trying to replicate Blockbuster's success in stocking the most popular videos was working on the wrong problem. What customers have always cared about is how to access the broadest selection of movies quickly and at the lowest cost. Netflix discovered that the new answer was digital streaming of videos over the Internet.

A very different example comes from the pharmaceutical industry. Pharmaceutical companies need to discover more new drugs faster. These companies have a narrow window of time to profit from their discoveries because the new drug discovery and FDA approval process can take forever, while the patent on these drugs is limited to 17 years. Just when they get to market with a successful new drug, they worry about the day they'll need to compete with generic drugs when their patent expires. Every day they can eliminate from the drug discovery and approval process is an additional day of profitability. The stakes are high since new drug discovery is an expensive undertaking with no guarantee of returns. Because of this, the drug discovery problem has attracted a wide range of solutions for decades: software to manage the FDA approval process, services to find clinical trial participants, and startups willing to sell the rights to their discoveries, to name a few. A promising new approach is to replace the experimental "wet lab" approach to drug discovery with an analytical approach based on supercomputer analysis of the human genome. The key to success is to focus not on the technology but on the problem: faster discovery and approval of effective new drugs.

Perhaps you're familiar with the story of Albert Einstein's final exam for his Princeton graduate students. The proctor who handed out the exam panicked when he realized that the questions were the same as the questions from the previous year's final exam. "Don't worry," said Einstein calmly to the proctor, "the answers are *different* this year."

Being clear about the problem you solve can also provide rich insights into the competitive landscape. An incumbent that is worried about disruptive competitors needs to ask: "What are other ways customers can meet this need?" and "Who else is trying to solve this problem?" Will Google Docs displace Microsoft Office? Will Skype displace international phone calling? If you understand the business problem and have a relationship with the customer, you have an early warning system for potentially disruptive competitors; there's no need to be surprised.

Figure 6.4: The Next Tool—Design.

Ultimately, the lesson is this: if you want to kick-start the innovation process, get your team out of the office to learn from customers. Finding the *next* problem to solve, before others do, can open up a new, uncontested market opportunity. Designing a better customer experience can be a source of competitive advantage more valuable than patents. Turn that newly discovered customer problem into a *design challenge*—and then you're ready for the next Innovation Power Tool: design.

CHAPTER HIGHLIGHTS

- The primary source of innovation is to learn the unmet and unarticulated needs of customers—ahead of competitors
- To uncover these needs companies need to spend time out of the office observing and listening.
- Good listening requires customer empathy—the ability to stand in the shoes of the customer—a skill that many executives need to develop.
- Don't expect customers to define the solution—that's the company's job in the design phase.

7

SOLVE PROBLEMS
LIKE A DESIGNER

NO BOUNDARIES

"Let's get started, everyone," Meena shouted to a room that sounded more like a cocktail party than a business meeting. "We've got a lot to cover over the next two days."

Meena had assembled NaviMark's leadership team for a two-day offsite at the Cambridge Innovation Center (CIC) in Kendall Square. They took their seats in the large Charles River Conference Room on the fourteenth floor overlooking MIT's Sloan School of Management and the Charles River. The CIC was a hotbed of startup activity in the greater Boston area—the headquarters for hundreds of small startups along with the venture capitalists, bankers, marketers, and other service providers who specialized in helping early stage ventures. NaviMark had spent its first two years on the eleventh floor of the CIC, not far from where Jack Huong still kept his office. Kapur hoped the familiar environment would set the tone: a return to the fundamentals of the business.

"Our agenda today is to get clear about where we want to take the business over the next two to three years. Then tomorrow we'll focus on next year's operating plan to make sure we know how to get there. I want to walk out of here tomorrow with a clear set of action items to get the

business back on track. I've asked Bill Kruse to run the meeting so I can participate in all of the discussions. And Jack Huong has agreed to join us. I guess the venture business must be slow this week," she said as she flashed a big smile to the company's original investor.

Bill took the team through a brief overview of the challenges facing NaviMark.

"There's been a recent gap between the growth targets you've shared with your board and the current trajectory of the business. If you just keep doing the same things, you're not going to get to an IPO in two years. In fact you may never establish yourselves as a market leader if you can't grow faster than your market." Bill looked around the room to make sure he wasn't competing with any laptops or smart phones. "The good news is that there are a number of really promising options for growing the company. The bad news is: there are way too many of these options. You'll need to make some choices. But first I want to make sure you explore all of the options.

"You've heard me talk about how revenues in companies like yours follow the shape of an S-Curve. It seems that the S-Curve for NaviMark's current product is starting to flatten. I think there are ways that NaviMark can stretch this curve and get a lot more growth by finding better ways to market the Navigator. And, of course, you have no choice because Navi-Mark doesn't have a new S-Curve to fall back on—not yet anyway. The RT technology is very exciting but you still don't have a finished product or a clear plan for where to sell it." He glanced at Tim Wiggins who was doing all he could to contain himself during these introductory comments.

"I've organized the group into two teams. The job of the Navigator Team is to identify new ways to generate revenue with the current Navigator product. Your goal is to outline a plan to achieve at least 50 percent annual growth over the next three years. The job of the RT Team is to define the target market and value proposition for the RT technology: who is the customer and what business problem will we solve? Your goal is to describe a line of business that will contribute at least 25 percent of NaviMark's revenues within three years.

"I've assigned a leader for each team, outlined a process for generating and evaluating various strategic options, and provided a set of ground rules. Fortunately, we have some fresh insights from customer interviews conducted over the last few weeks by three teams of executives that will provide a good starting point. Let's reconvene at 2:00 PM to review the progress of the two teams."

Bill spent the next hour listening to the Navigator team, which remained in the main meeting room. After reviewing the findings of the customer research, the team created an updated profile of the Navigator customer and discussed the reasons these customers were buying the Navigator product. They created a list of business applications the Navigator could address and discussed the value of each of these applications to their customer. They also reviewed the latest sales pipeline and an analysis of why they had won or lost important deals.

"We're selling ourselves short," said Raj. "Our customers don't seem to understand how much better they can target their marketing dollars. If you're running marketing, the way to become a hero is to generate more high-quality leads."

"Maybe we haven't done a good job of explaining how the Navigator is designed to do this," said Kemi.

"Have we thought about creating our own professional services team to help customize the Navigator setup for each different business?" said Jack. "Professional services alone could account for 10 to 15 percent of NaviMark revenues."

"Do we really want to get into professional services?" said Raj. "I mean, wouldn't that drag down our valuation multiples?"

"Time out," said Patrick. "We're in the idea generation stage of our process. We'll have plenty of time to evaluate some of these ideas later. Right now I'm interested in more ideas. Kemi, did you have another suggestion?"

Bill could see that the Navigator Team was in good hands and spent the next hour with the RT Team that was meeting in the Fenway Conference Room.

"My big question is, 'Are we a marketing services company, or an analytics company?'" said Tina Thorn. "We've been telling the market that we help generate more leads with fewer dollars. I don't know what this has to do with robots and manufacturing?"

"I don't want to spoil the party here but who said we know anything about generating leads?" said Meena. "I mean really, we don't even know how to generate leads for ourselves. Wasn't lead generation simply a market we went after because marketers don't do a great job of analyzing and optimizing their marketing spending? We might have chosen energy management if we thought there was a big enough market."

"Whoa, energy management. Now there's an interesting market," said Tim.

"However we got here, I think marketing analytics turned out to be a good market to tackle," said Anthony. "And I think there are some interesting big-data problems that we can help marketers solve."

"Eventually, yes. But how long will that market take to develop? I want to make sure we find the fastest path to new revenues . . . while we're young," said Meena.

"OK, why don't we generate a couple of different lists of options," said Tim. "The first would include all of the marketing applications that we could tackle with our RT technology. This assumes we would keep our vertical focus on marketing and sell more to the customers we know. The second list would include other business applications beyond marketing that require sophisticated analytics. If we went in this direction we would be more of a general purpose or horizontal platform that could be customized for many different applications—the Swiss Army Knife of big data analytics."

"Let's start with the second list and work our way back to marketing applications," Kemi suggested. "I'm happy to start. So in addition to robotics and manufacturing automation, which we've discussed, I think we should explore the life sciences industry. There's a revolution in drug discovery and disease treatment going on using genetics research. The amount of data involved is staggering—one human genome is equivalent to about three gigabytes of data. And Boston is in the epicenter of

this revolution; we have the early adopter hospitals, the research and academic community, the data scientists, the investors, and some successful life sciences companies. We need to engage with this community and find the best way to flex our analytical muscles."

"I think that's an interesting sector. I've got another one," Patrick chimed in. "Hedge funds. The stock traders that people refer to as 'quants' have big budgets for any tools that might give them an edge in trading stocks and commodities: pork bellies, oil, micro-cap companies, precious metals—whatever they want to trade. I think they'd really like our dashboard."

"What about environmental modeling?" Anthony added. "We might develop better applications for weather forecasting, or siting and managing wind farms. It might also tie into the hedge fund markets; if you understand how weather patterns will affect energy demand, you might make some smart trades in the spot markets for oil."

"Could we tie that into energy management?" said Patrick. "We could help utilities make decisions about purchasing power from the grid, or buying coal, oil, or natural gas. We might also help make sense of all of the electric metering data that's collected every minute of the day from businesses and consumers. You can save a lot of money on electricity production during periods of peak demand if you can charge higher prices or get people to turn off some appliances."

Bill liked the flow of the conversation. "I'm going to spend time with the other team. Let me first make a couple of suggestions. For each of the markets you identify, please make clear who the buyer would be and what business problem you would solve for them. Also, once you've flushed out all of the options, please rank-order them, and then pick your top two ideas to present to the other team. I'll be back."

DESIGN THINKING

Design thinking is a different approach to solving complex problems.

Most managers are trained to make decisions: identify the options, analyze the pros and cons, determine the present value of each option, consider

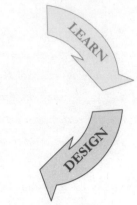

Figure 7.1: Power Innovation Tool—Design.

the risk factors, and, in any case, choose the best option—because every manager *knows* that it's better to make some kind of decision and move forward than to fail to take action.

Designers don't think this way. Presented with the same set of options, a designer is likely to say, "How do we know these are the best options?" The designer's instinct will be to ask a lot of questions about the problem and then search for new, better options without stressing over the deadline. This, of course, drives decision makers crazy because, "*we already know what the options are and we're running out of time.*" But the designer believes there may be an option that is so compelling that you won't need a lot of analyses to know it's the best solution. Albert Einstein once said, "It's not that I'm so smart. It's just that I stay with problems longer."[1]

The way designers solve problems is called *design thinking.* It's an approach that's particularly well suited to unstructured, one-of-a-kind problems. Design thinking involves several important steps. First, develop a deep, human-centered understanding of the customer and their issues in order to define the *design challenge,* that is, the problem you want to solve. Second, use any number of expansive, creative thinking processes to generate a wide range of possible solutions. Third, choose the best solutions and test them with prospective customers.

Designers have used this approach for a long time, in architecture, product design, fashion, and other creative fields. In recent years, however, design thinking has made its way into the world of business. A new generation of design consultants uses this approach to help clients with new product development, business model innovation, and growth strategy. Not to be outdone—or disrupted—traditional business consulting firms are adding designers to their staffs; Accenture, for example, acquired the design consultancy Fjord. Progressive universities such as Stanford and Northwestern are promoting design-thinking collaborations across their liberal arts, science, business, and engineering departments. In 2008, the California School of Arts introduced the Design Strategy MBA, the first graduate school focused on the intersection of design and business.[2] Venture capital leader Kleiner Perkins created a three-month fellowship for talented designers with the hope of recruiting them for their promising startups.

Companies are adding designers to their product teams. Box, the collaboration software upstart, is taking on Microsoft, Citrix, Google, and others largely on the basis of the ease of use of its products, thanks to a team of seven user interface designers and eleven brand designers. CEO Aaron Levie explains, "I think we're uniquely positioned as a company that can take a lot of the design focus that you'd see in a consumer company and bring it to the enterprise."[3] The most influential product strategist at Apple—after Steve Jobs of course—has been Jonathan Ive, a classically trained industrial designer recruited by Jobs to bring design thinking to Apple. Ive was the lead designer for the MacBook, iPod, iPhone, and iPad, and other great Apple products. Along the way, he built an elite team of design specialists who secretly work on Apple's next-generation products. What will Apple's next breakthrough product be—a smart wristwatch or perhaps some other wearable technology?[4]

DESIGN TOOLS

Design thinking is an approach, not a prescriptive methodology. Still there are helpful problem-solving frameworks that designers use; these differ from traditional decision tools used by *decision thinkers*.

Decision Tools	Design Tools
Segmentation	Empathy Map
Value Chain	Journey Map
SWOT	User Narrative

Figure 7.2: Decision and Design Tools.

Decision tools use an analytical approach to converge on the *right* answer—like assembling the pieces to solve a big puzzle. In particular, strategy frameworks help companies improve their competitive advantage and optimize their market share; these tools assume that a market exists with established competitors. Kim and Mauborgne, authors of *Blue Ocean Strategy,* call this the *red ocean* because established markets are full of competitive sharks.[5] Among the best known red ocean tools are: market segmentation, used to find more efficient ways to serve established markets; value chain analysis, used to decide where to develop competencies and what to outsource; and the time-honored SWOT analysis, used to take inventory of a situation—strengths, weaknesses, opportunities, and threats—before deciding where to take action.

Designers use tools intended to solve unstructured problems in markets that may not exist. How can we reduce the number of vehicle miles traveled in the city of Boston? How can we reduce by 80 percent the time it takes to train our customers? You can find a collection of design tools in *Designing for Growth* and *Gamestorming,* but three versatile frameworks to start with are the empathy map, the customer journey map, and the user narrative.

Design teams use the empathy map to distill their findings from customer interviews. Often taped to a wall where individuals can add comments on yellow Post-It notes, the teams use this map to search for patterns with the hope of uncovering promising new problems to solve. To create an empathy map, you start with a profile of the target customer: role, title, age, demographics, and other characteristics. Use a drawing or photo of a typical customer if it helps. You then try to capture what it's like to be this

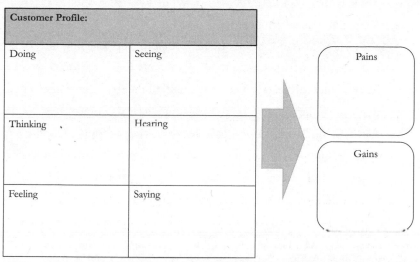

Figure 7.3: Standing in the Shoes of the Customer. Source: Adapted by Author from Dave Gray, Sunni Brown, and James Macanufo, Gamestorming *(Sebastapol, CA: O'Reilly Media, 2010), 65.*

customer by describing their world as they perceive it—what do they see, do, hear, and say?

Using this rich factual and emotional profile of the customer, the design team identifies opportunities to address customer *pains* and *gains*. Pains are problems the customer needs to solve: demands from *their* customers, budget and time constraints, products and services that don't work as advertised, obstacles to progress, and career risks. Gains are upside opportunities: the ability to do more with less, an unexpected new capability that changes the way they get their work done, an opportunity to innovate, a career development opportunity.

Design teams hope to synthesize the pains and gains into a design challenge—a crisp statement of a customer problem worth solving. The design challenge is not a description of the solution—it defines the mission of the design team. For James Dyson it was: how can I make a consumer vacuum cleaner with enough suction to get the job done? For Darn Tough Socks: how can I make a sock that's both comfortable and durable enough for outdoor sports athletes? The design challenge provides the necessary goals, focus, and boundaries for the creative work that follows. Who wants to work on a problem that no one cares about? What business wants to invest in technology-in-search-of-a-market?

Another design tool that's particularly helpful for designing great customer experiences in either B2C or B2B markets is the customer journey map. To construct this map you first lay out all of the steps a customer would go through from the moment they realize they have a problem to the time when they're happily using a new product or service: shopping, purchasing, learning to use the product, getting answers to support questions, renewing a subscription, and so on. If you plan to disrupt this market with a completely new offer, or improve an existing offer, you want to eliminate all of the friction in this process and shrink the time from *recognized need* to *satisfied customer* to as close to zero as possible. Travel services companies use this approach to improve the door-to-door experiences of business and consumer travelers.

Once you've outlined the steps in the process that are unique to your customer and product or service category, you describe the customer experiences at each stage of the journey. What's it like for a customer in this market to find a solution once they realize they have a need? What's the purchasing process like—do they need to stand in line, meet with a sales rep, fill out forms? Once they've purchased the product or service, how quickly can they start using it—is there assembly required, is training available, is it

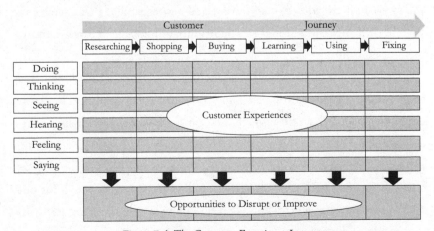

Figure 7.4: The Customer Experience Journey.

push-button-simple to use? By breaking down the process as the customer experiences it, companies can generate a list of design challenges or action items to address bottlenecks in the process. The next step is to prioritize these customer problems and then begin to design a better—often disruptive experience. This is the approach that Zappos used to dominate online shoe sales. Imagine how many industries you could transform using this approach.

The empathy map and the customer experience journey help companies think differently, and empathetically, about customer problems. These simple frameworks never become obsolete because customer problems are always changing. And if *empathy map* sounds a little too touchy-feely for your company, call it a *customer workflow analysis* and ask your team what customers are complaining about.

A powerful way to summarize a team's hypotheses about the customer problem to solve—the design challenge—is to create an end user narrative. This is a *story* about the customer, his or her situation, and what gives rise to the need for a new solution. The narrative describes the kind of customer experience that the solution should deliver. Unlike a traditional market requirements document (MRD) this narrative creates a vision of the desired solution in the context of the user. It provides a vivid customer profile that can put all members of the design team on the same page. Howard Schultz wanted to bring the experience of the European coffee bar to the United States; Steve Jobs wanted to put your entire music library in your pocket. The designers took over from there.

CREATING NEW DESIGN OPTIONS

Once you've decided on the design challenge, you need to develop a range of options for solving the problem. This is the stage most often associated with creativity and brainstorming because the best solutions are not obvious—otherwise someone would have already solved the problem. Here are a few basics on this rich topic.

A simple description of the creative process is to combine unrelated ideas until you turn up a valuable new solution. *Unrelated* ideas because if the ideas were already related a solution would likely exist. If you have a technical background you can think of the creative process as a kind of matching engine: the more unrelated ideas you can match in a given amount of time, the better the chances that a valuable new solution will reveal itself. The process is largely trial-and-error, and it takes time.

There are several ways to ensure that your problem solving or creative process has a rich supply of unrelated ideas. One is to assemble a problem-solving team that brings a wide range of experiences from different domains that are at least loosely related to the design challenge. This is why you see design team members with backgrounds in engineering, finance, marketing, psychology, science, education, and other disciplines. A melting pot of a team like this not only brings unrelated ideas to the table but also provides an expanded set of pattern-recognition skills to spot the valuable combinations when they emerge. I can only imagine the kind of design team it took to create the Rosetta Stone software system for learning a new language by pointing to pictures.

The process that a problem-solving team goes through to generate new options has three stages: expand, explore, and choose.

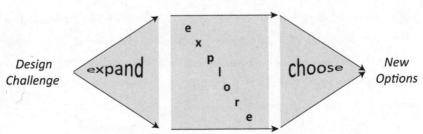

Figure 7.5: Creating New Options. Source: Adapted by Author from Dave Gray, Sunni Brown, and James Macanufo, Gamestorming *(Sebastopol, CA: O'Reilly Media, 2010), 12.*

EXPAND: The process begins by having the new product team understand the design challenge and then generate a wide range of possibilities. The more ideas you can generate early on, the more raw material you have to work with when exploring and finally choosing the best ideas. This is analogous to unqualified leads going into a pipeline; the more leads the better. Team members first generate ideas individually, then as a group.

For individuals generating ideas, one guideline from the Stanford d.school is to write down at least 50 ideas. This may seem like a lot, but the process of generating this many ideas forces you to move past the obvious solutions and to search for new ways to think about the problem.[6]

Innovation expert Kaihan Krippendorf observes that too many companies stop at three options when solving a problem. The innovators, he argues, push for what he calls *The 4th Option,* one that is not obvious and that is more likely to become the source of competitive advantage. To help companies get outside the box to discover new options he draws on a collection of ancient Chinese stratagems. Each of 36 phrases such as "Kill with the borrowed knife" and "Exchange a brick for a jade" suggests a generic strategy that is intended to trigger a new approach to an intractable business problem.[7]

In a group process you need ground rules and a facilitator. One important ground rule is to minimize any critical comments in the early stages of the process. If you have someone in the room saying "we tried that before," or "you've got to be kidding," it dampens the creative mood. Another ground rule is to build on the ideas that others have. You want to take advantage of the diverse talent in the room by having everyone listen to every idea with the hope that it sparks an entirely new idea. A facilitator can manage the process, enforce the ground rules, and keep track of the ideas. Because this process is unfamiliar—even anathema—to some decision thinkers, expect at least one participant in any group to say "I'm lost. What are we supposed to be doing now?" The facilitator needs the credibility and the experience to persuade participants to trust the process.

The process of generating ideas doesn't need to occur in one grand brainstorming big bang. There's no workflow process for inspiration. Ideas reveal themselves over time in customer meetings, while working out, on a plane, in a conversation with a business partner, and any number of other situations. Large companies are using collaboration software—Intuit Brainstorm, for example—to capture, share, and build on the ideas of their employees, whenever and wherever they occur around the world. With such a software tool an employee in Singapore can learn about an idea that some-one in New York generated several days ago, build on that idea based on a recent meeting she had, and add new insights that might be discovered several days later by an engineer in Dallas who is redesigning the product. It's brainstorming-meets-social-networking.

Hopefully, a number of the options that emerge from this process will be the kind of transformational, disruptive ideas that can lead to a new S-Curve. However, most of the ideas are likely to be incremental improve-ments to existing products and services that allow you to stretch the S-Curve. Both categories of ideas contribute to the company's growth strategy. But to be sure you get your fair share of the disruptive ideas, the front end of the process must have enough customer insights, team diversity, and expansive thinking to create those new combinations of unrelated ideas that lead to breakthroughs.

EXPLORE: Brainstorming has a bad reputation. Many view it as throwing spaghetti against the wall to see what sticks. But the process shouldn't end with a large number of partially baked ideas. The best ideas need further baking.

The new product team first needs to select a few ideas and develop them. Often the best ideas are obvious; if not, the team might simply vote on the two or three ideas they want to explore in more depth. For each of these contenders they need to ask, "If we went in this direction, what would it look like?" Each of these promising ideas might be assigned to a different team to flush out over a period of days or weeks.

Many companies known for their product innovations commission mul-tiple, competing product teams to take an independent approach to the same design challenge or market opportunity. The idea of a design competition is not new. The Renaissance began in 1401 with a competition to design bronze doors for the Baptistery of San Giovanni in Florence. Although Ghiberti won the bronze door commission, finalist Brunelleschi won a second competition to design one of the great architectural works of the Renaissance—the dome of the Santa Maria del Fiore cathedral in the center of Florence. In 1714, the British Parliament issued the Longitude Prize to find a solution to one of the most dangerous hazards for ships at sea: not knowing your longitude and therefore how far you are from shore. A modern day analogy would be XPrize, a foundation that gives awards to teams who solve the most "impossible problems," including space exploration, oil spill cleanup, personal health monitoring, and automotive fuel efficiency. For growth stage companies, a practical approach to design competition might be to assign separate teams to flush out two or three competing designs.

Some companies will outsource a part of the design process to a design firm such as IDEO, which helped Apple design its original computer mouse, or Continuum, which designed the Swiffer for Procter and Gamble. You can also use the Internet to *crowdsource* a new design by issuing a design challenge to all comers in cyberspace. Topcoder provides access to over 500,000 independent software developers to work on a software design problem you may have; NASA, Humana, and the Harvard Medical School have used Topcoder's *enterprise open innovation* process.

CHOOSE: There comes a point in any innovation process when you need to make choices. The process is fueled not only by a great design challenge but also by constraints. To design without constraints isn't much of a challenge. With unlimited time and money you can design almost anything . . . or nothing at all.

Deadlines create important milestones that require teams to choose the best ideas before moving forward. Venture capital firms don't provide the money it would take to build a company; they *stage* the financing to provide just enough time and capital for a team to prove they can get to the next stage of a project: a proof-of-concept, a first customer, or a workable business model.

Choosing is the step that's missing in many creative efforts. It's the step that moves brainstorming from "spaghetti on the wall" to good ideas worth developing further. But choosing at this stage is not an irreversible decision. It's simply the starting point for another set of interactions with customers to *test* whether they're interested in any of these ideas.

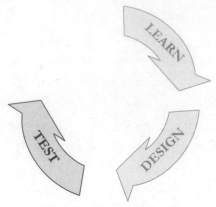

Figure 7.6: The Next Tool—Test.

CHAPTER HIGHLIGHTS

- Uncovering new growth opportunities is an unstructured problem that requires a different approach—design thinking.
- Design thinking takes a human-centric approach to discover the unarticulated needs of customers, and translate these needs into new solutions.
- Empathy maps, customer journey maps, and user narratives are among the most effective tools that designers use in this process.
- The design process has several stages: diverge, explore, and decide. It's important to manage each stage the right way to get the best results.

8

FEEDBACK IS A GIFT

SNEAK PREVIEW

"Please have a seat and we'll get started," said NaviMark's VP of Marketing, Patrick Howard, as he prepared to demonstrate a prototype of LoyalOne. Assembled in the VIP Suite at the Hyatt Grand Cypress in Orlando were four marketing executives in town for Loyalty Expo, an annual conference for the customer loyalty industry. Patrick was using this conference to solicit feedback on an early release of a new NaviMark product. It was an effective and inexpensive way to gather informal feedback from this highly specialized segment of marketers. The VIP Suite was cheaper than setting up a booth at the trade show—and more private.

"LoyalOne helps you drive more repeat purchases from your best customers," Patrick began. "Using sophisticated analytics, it learns the buying behavior of repeat purchasers and then identifies customers who should be buying more. Let me show you how it works."

After a 20-minute presentation, Patrick asked the marketing executives for their reactions.

"Lose the name," said one executive as the other three chuckled. "Every time I see a product with the word 'loyal' in the name, my eyes glaze over."

"It's just a placeholder name," said Patrick defensively. He knew that naming a product was just about the hardest and most thankless job for a marketer. "But thanks for the feedback."

"Where do you get the data?" another executive asked. "I'm not sure we'd have what you need to run your analysis."

Albert Li took notes as Patrick fielded the questions. After another 20 minutes of discussion, he asked each of the executives a few of his own questions.

"How do you solve the problem of getting more repeat buyers in your business today?" Albert asked.

"We don't really have this problem," said one executive. "I just came for the Jambox." The room broke out in laughter; as an incentive for participating, every executive received a Jambox portable speaker. "Seriously, in our business we have the name of every business that buys our product and we have a group of marketing programs and reminders that we send to promote upgrades or new offers. There's not a lot of math involved."

"Good for you," said a second executive. "I wish I could say the same. Our problem is a little more complicated. We sell linens, towels, shower curtains, and other bed and bath products to homes, hospitals, and retailers. We sell our own brand online and we create private label versions for some of the big retailers. Lots of people want to buy an extra towel or pillowcase and can't find the right match. If we could do what you're describing we could make a lot more money."

A third executive leaned into the discussion. "Would this be a feature of the next release of Navigator or would we need to pay extra?"

"LoyalOne, or whatever we call it, would be a new module that you could 'snap-in' to the Navigator," said Patrick. "It would appear as a new drop-down menu on your screen. Here's the proposed pricing." Patrick pulled up a slide that showed the preliminary pricing schedule.

"Hmm," was the only response as the customer thought about the pricing and packaging approach. "Will you be providing services to help us customize this LoyalOne module for our business?"

At the end of the 90-minute discussion about customer loyalty challenges at each of the three businesses, Patrick and Albert thanked the executives for participating and made arrangements to continue the dialogue as they created a final version of their customer loyalty solution.

"Well," said Albert. "That was eye opening. I'm glad we didn't create anything more than screen shots of this concept."

"Speaking of which," said Patrick as he sat in front of his laptop, "let's change the name before the next group gets here."

"Is it working?" Tim Wiggins asked as he stared at the large monitor in the control room of the robotics test lab.

"Just give it a second. It's thinking," said Jon Storm, one of NaviMark's senior engineers, as he waited nervously for the results of his demo.

Tim Wiggins had convinced TCS Electronics and two other manufacturing companies to become design partners, helping NaviMark to develop a new robotic control solution using its big-data analytical tools. These manufacturers had also persuaded Rearden Automation, the company whose robots they both used, to collaborate in the project. The partnership with Rearden made it easier for NaviMark to access the data and underlying control systems it needed to make its solution work. The Rearden executives were excited enough about the project that they made space available in their test lab in Worcester, Massachusetts. If this new solution could make Rearden's robots more productive, NaviMark could gain a valuable distribution partner.

"There. We just got Robot Number 5 to change the way it assembles that component by learning from the mistakes of the other robots. That's pretty good, I think."

"We'll let our design partners be the judge of that," said Tim, "but I'm impressed. What just happened anyway?"

"We connected our analytics engine to the Rearden control panel that monitors the robots as they go through their assembly routines. These routines are programmed by operations engineers based on each company's manufacturing process; right now we're using an assembly routine that TSC Electronics gave us. After a while it became clear that certain steps in the process weren't working as well—the number of defects increased and you could see bottlenecks appear in the workflow. Normally the operations engineers pick up on these problems and make *small adjustments to the robots over the course of a few days or weeks. However in this demonstration our software found the problem within an hour and then ran a pretty sophisticated artificial intelligence program that 'automagically' reprogrammed the robots. Pretty slick, eh?"*

"Where did you find the artificial intelligence software?" Tim asked.

"It's a free, open source software program called Mentor9 that programmers have been using for years to analyze behavior patterns. It's a pretty robust artificial intelligence program that's embedded in many applications. It was used in the gaming application that beat a professional Texas hold'em champion last year."

"Does Albert know you're using open source software in this prototype?" asked Tim.

"Uhh . . . I'm not sure we'd use Mentor9 in the commercial version of this product," the engineer responded sheepishly. "But it was the cheapest and fastest way to get the demo working."

Tim saw that he had a call from Luisa Ruiz of TSC Electronics. "Did you see that, Tim?" said Luiza. "That was amazing. We've been watching the demo on Skype. How do we get this to be a real product?"

Tim wondered how NaviMark had gotten so deeply involved in a solution involving robots and manufacturing—using software that could outsmart poker players. It was a pivot to an entirely new direction for the company. And one thing was clear: he had paying customers and an eager business partner if he could make all of this work. After a tough few months, he was feeling more positive about NaviMark's prospects than ever. It would take some effort to get the board comfortable with these new developments. But he'd rely on Meena to do that.

TEST

No one gets it right the first time.

In 1998, Confinity started out as a cryptography company whose goal was to allow Palm Pilot users to make wireless payments. Its application would allow a Palm user to *beam* money to another mobile device using the Pilot's built-in infrared signal. Two years later, a struggling Confinity merged

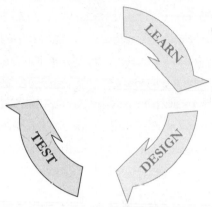

Figure 8.1. Innovation Power Tool—Test.

with X.Com, a nearby Palo Alto company that focused on electronic payments via e-mail. The merged company discovered a growing market of eBay users who wanted to exchange money securely over the Internet; it turned out that X.Com's payment system, called *PayPal,* was more popular than eBay's own payment solution. X.Com went public as PayPal in 2000; five months later eBay acquired PayPal for $1.5 billion.[1]

Mark Zuckerberg's success was far from assured when he launched Facemash.com, a site that allowed students to see pictures of other students and vote on who was "hot" or "not." Before his site was shut down—for hacking the Harvard network to get student photos—the traffic he generated told Zuckerberg a great deal about student behavior and the power of photos.

It's smart to test your ideas early with a few customers to see if you're on track. Getting customer feedback early allows you to improve your design, get to market earlier with the *right* product, and avoid investing a lot of money in a colossal failure.

About the time that X.Com was becoming PayPal, WebVan was losing hundreds of millions of dollars trying to create a home delivery service for groceries. WebVan bet on a national rollout of its concept, taking the company public to fund continuing losses, and reportedly placing orders for more than $1 billion to build warehouses and buy computers. The company soon went out of business. But WebVan might have found a business model that worked by concentrating on its original market, the San Francisco Bay Area; experts believed that learning to target high-density neighborhoods was the key to profitability. Indeed, some grocery chains have since found a way to make the home delivery model work.[2]

Market testing is a way to learn as early as possible, and as cheaply as possible, what it will take to succeed with customers. The key is to start the testing process earlier than you think. And to do the testing, you need a *prototype*.

PROTOTYPING

A prototype is an incomplete, early version of a product or service that helps answer the questions: "How will it work?" and "Is this what customers want?" Good prototyping is a form of impressionism, creating just enough of a representation of the new offer to allow you to gather meaningful customer feedback. Sometimes customers need to squint.

Prototypes come in many forms. Architects build scale models of their building designs. Product designers create mock-ups of product ideas. Software companies create alpha versions of their software (that's one step *before* the beta version). Some entrepreneurs win investors over with drawings on the back of a napkin. Movie producers create storyboards. The key to prototyping is to keep it low resolution and simple; don't make a science project out of it. You want to uncover design flaws, faulty assumptions, and unexpected problems. You also want to clarify what a customer is really looking for: *"Would a solution like this address the problem you described?"*

Technology has made prototyping a lot easier. With a few well-designed screen shots and some clever animation you can illustrate how a web application would work and get feedback on the look and feel of the user experience. Product designers who prefer physical representations of their designs can now use design software and 3D printers to create three-dimensional models of their prototypes that customers can hold in their hands. Virtual reality technology lets companies simulate a new product or service in cyberspace, allowing customers to consider: "What would it be like to walk around the inside of the new building?" or "What would I look like wearing that outfit?"

Long before eBay was big enough to buy PayPal for $1.5 billion, its founder, Pierre Omidyar, created a simple prototype to test his vision. He imagined a world in which anyone could buy anything in a global marketplace. He created a simple website where he listed for sale a broken laser pointer. When a buyer for the used device showed up at his website, he knew he was on the right track.

Jeff Bezos had a more complex vision to test. Rather than simply connecting buyers and sellers online like eBay, he wanted to be a retailer without owning stores. After a careful analysis of all the products he might sell on an e-commerce site, he chose books as his starting point. He then designed a prototype that would remind you more of a lemonade stand than Amazon. com. He listed books for sale on his website and waited to see if people would buy them (remember that buying anything online was unheard of in 1995). When he got his first orders he would buy the books from a distributor, wrap them, and ship them. Not much of a business model but a great proof of concept to validate the market.

Fast-forward to today and authors are now leveraging the large community of Amazon readers to do their own prototyping. In 2011 Hugh Howey wrote a short story about a future in which earth's remaining inhabitants live in a silo underground. He published *Wool* on Amazon for 99 cents. Surprised by the positive response from readers he wrote a sequel that also sold well. He then wrote and sold three more chapters, and finally a Kindle book combining the first five installments that he sold for $5.99. To build momentum for *Wool,* Howey sent free copies to bloggers who reviewed books, and encouraged his fans to contribute book art and review early drafts. *Wool* went on to become a national bestseller and may yet become a movie—and all because of the success of Howey's short story prototype.[3]

Prototyping is enjoying a renaissance among growth companies thanks to the efforts of Steve Blank and Eric Ries, both entrepreneurs and authors who have promoted a "lean" approach to building businesses. The lean movement started in the software industry where development experts learned that small teams building and testing software programs one module at a time could outperform large teams building complete applications all at once. Product managers applied these *lean* concepts to the market development process: define the problem, build a small prototype, test with customers, repeat. Ries recast the prototype as a *minimum viable product,* also known by its acronym, *MVP.* The MVP is the most basic version of a new product concept. It's just enough of a prototype to get meaningful customer feedback; any further investment would be wasted effort until you learn more about what customers really want. (The concept applies to service companies as well; some companies use the term *minimum viable solution* or *MVS.*)

How minimum can the minimum viable product be? In the case of Dropbox, the web service that allows users to share and store computer files, the MVP was a YouTube video.

Drew Houston, the founder of Dropbox, wanted to validate his idea for an Internet file-sharing service before he raised capital and threw himself into a startup. The file-sharing market was already crowded with competitors but none offered an easy-to-use solution; the Dropbox tagline: *It Just Works.* Before taking on the risk and complexity of building a working solution, he created a video that illustrated how his product was intended to work—with a particular focus on the customer experience. This video made its way to Y Combinator, the incubator that provided angel funding for the business. A year later, Houston released a second video on *Digg,* the tech news site, to attract early adopters for an early release of Dropbox; the response was overwhelmingly positive. Said Houston at the time: "It drove hundreds of thousands of people to the website. Our beta waiting list went from 5,000 people to 75,000 people literally overnight. It totally blew us away."[4]

Mitch Harper, co-founder of Bigcommerce, used a blog to get real-time feedback from lead users on the first version of the company's e-commerce product. Every few days he would post a blog describing a new module—including screen shots or a video—and then solicit comments. Here is an excerpt from a typical blog post:

THE BIGCOMMERCE BLOG:
WHY SHOULD SHIPPING BE SO HARD?

Mitch Harper: I've looked at a *lot* of e-commerce solutions and the one thing that 99.99% of them lack is usability. Today I just wanted to share a few screenshots with you that demonstrate how shipping integration will work in Bigcommerce.

Comment #1 (Posted by KZ): Nice, nice, looks to be easy to use and understand.

Comment #2 (Posted by DB): How would you handle selling software in your shopping cart if the purchased software is for download only?

Mitch Harper: Hi DB. Bigcommerce supports both physical and downloadable products. If you only sell downloadable products it skips the shipping step. Hope this helps.

Harper started the blog by reaching out to customers of Bigcommerce's e-mail marketing product. Over time, the list of followers grew to more than 250,000 because he provided useful information about online marketing techniques, responded to every comment (which is unusual for a company founder), and incorporated suggestions from lead users into the new product. By the time the e-commerce product shipped, Bigcommerce had 10,000 customers—many of them web designers with multiple clients needing a shopping cart.[5]

Not every test result is a runaway success like DropBox or Bigcommerce. At some point a failed test may mean there's not a market worth pursuing, and that it's time to move on. Three serial entrepreneurs from Boston's software industry set out to start a new business based on Bluetooth technology. At the time, Bluetooth had been approved as a new protocol for wireless communication over short distances (like connecting an earpiece to a smart phone). They raised just enough seed capital to fund a six-month search for an innovation. Rather than writing code, they used their funding for extensive field research with prospective business customers. They sifted through the best ideas and settled on the most promising concept: a smart device for shopping in retail stores. They created a prototype that consisted of sample screen shots on a smartphone. After a number of meetings with larger retailers it became clear that there was no market for their application. The entrepreneurs, and the investor who backed them, were disappointed with the outcome but satisfied with the process. They had given it their best shot and were now ready to pursue other ideas.

It's amazing how many companies give short shrift to the prototyping stage of the innovation process. Some may believe it's a distraction that will diminish their time-to-market advantage—but these individuals are focusing on the wrong kind of advantage. Getting to market first with the wrong product is not worth the effort. Competitive strategists would be better off replacing the term *time-to-market* with the less elegantly worded phrase: *time-to-market-with-the-right-product*. Here prototyping can make all the difference. Others who avoid the discipline of prototyping may be uncomfortable asking busy customers to give them feedback on an unfinished product. They worry about sending a message that the company has lowered its quality standards. While every market has its *trailing-edge* customers who are only interested in the finished product, there are always *early adopters* who welcome the opportunity to learn about and shape the development of new products. These are customers who look past the flaws and missing features to consider the possibilities. The key is to cultivate these visionary customers and engage them in your innovation process.

Some companies recruit early adopters to focus groups. If you want feedback on a new mobile application, invite college students to a convenient location in exchange for a free lunch. You'll be amazed at what you can learn for a limited investment of time and money; one mobile payment startup watched a group of college students create an advertising campaign that was far more effective than the mockups from its advertising agency. Other companies create customer advisory boards that meet periodically and provide practical feedback in exchange for an opportunity to network with their colleagues and enjoy dinner at a fine restaurant.

Google has found a different way to engage early adopters. It releases beta versions of new applications like Google+ and prototypes of new product concepts like Google Glass. Gmail and Google Docs began as beta products before becoming mainstream offers. The first prototype of Google Glass was constructed in one day using a coat hanger, leftover plexiglass, a plastic sheet protector, a wire harness and a netbook. Google doesn't pretend to know what the killer app will be; it hopes that users will find applications that no one had dreamed of. If not, it's back to the drawing board.[6]

What do companies do with all the feedback from a well-designed prototype? They *pivot*.

PIVOTING

To pivot is to try again—with the benefit of some learning. In golf, this would be a mulligan; in baseball, another at bat. The more opportunities you have to pivot, and the shorter the intervals between pivots, the better your chances of finding success. Some call this the *mathematics of innovation.*[7]

Although Groupon raced quickly to the end of its first S-Curve the company is not content to let its large franchise go stale; two-thirds of Groupon customers make another purchase within six months. A new CEO, Eric Lefkofsky, *pivoted* Groupon away from its tired model of e-mailing daily deals to a mobile-centric model where users can search for deals when they're feeling adventurous. He also acquired a company to launch a new Groupon service for making restaurant reservations.[8] Lefkofsky's pivots paid off as Groupon's stock price more than doubled during 2013.

Many startups pivot their way to success. YouTube started as a dating site. Twitter started as a podcast-sharing site named Odeo. Flickr began as a massive online gaming site. The key is not to run out of pivots before you run out of capital.

Most venture capitalists will tell you that they don't rely on the business plans that entrepreneurs present to them. In an early stage business so little is known about the market that no one can develop an accurate three-year revenue forecast, let alone predict how customers will respond to the new

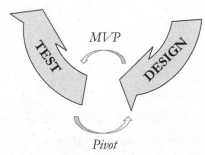

Pivot

Figure 8.2: MVP and Pivot.

offer. The business plan is more of a written exam that demonstrates how entrepreneurs think about developing a new offer and making money. Even the best business plans can become obsolete before the company gets its first round of funding. What VCs look for is a learning team—that is, a team that's prepared to get their MVP to market as quickly as possible, listen to customers, and keep pivoting until they succeed.

Steve Blank recommends that growth companies replace the term *product development* with *customer development*. His message to new product teams is to make sure you understand who the customer is and what problem you solve—using MVPs and pivots—before you waste time and money launching a product or building a business. His *Customer Development Manifesto* begins with a phrase that should be posted on the wall of every new product team: *"There are no facts inside your building, so get outside."*[9]

Pivots are not just random walks. Ries argues that companies should be testing hypotheses about the market and business model, and then pivoting in a way that retains the attractive elements of the strategy but changes the ineffective elements based on market feedback. Most stories of company pivots are full of revisionist history. Still, they're generally fun and inspiring. So here are three brief pivot stories to close the chapter.

In 2009 Ben Silbermann launched a mobile application called Tote whose mission was to make retail shopping easier. Users could scan items at Banana Republic, Anthropologie, and other retailers, save their favorite items, get alerts when these items were on sale, and find the nearest stores. So far, so good. But Tote lacked a workable payment solution, making it hard to live up to its retail shopping value proposition. What Tote discovered, while the lights were still on, was that it had built a large following of users that saved photos of their favorite collections—of clothes, books, pets, beverages, and other items. Silbermann decided to cater to this market as Pinterest, encouraging users to *pin* photos of their favorite collections . . . of anything.[10] In 2013, Pinterest had more than 50 million unique monthly visitors worldwide and had raised over $523 million from investors, putting the company's valuation at an impressive $3.8 billion.[11]

Pixar spun out of Lucasfilm to build production systems for creating digital animation. The company failed to get traction with its systems. To demonstrate the potential of its technology, Pixar created its own animation demos, including a critically acclaimed short about two lamps called *Luxo, Jr.* Pixar's owner, Steve Jobs, eventually sold the equipment part of the business to focus on movie production. Pixar landed a contract with Disney to produce three animation movies—one of which was *Toy Story*—and put digital animation on the map.

Pivoting is not just for startups. Witness Coca Cola's more recent approach to new product launches. New Coke has long been a poster child for failed product launches. A response to The Pepsi Challenge, this sweeter version of Coke was not what die-hard Coke fans wanted; Coca Cola was forced to drop New Coke and re-introduce Coke Classic. But Coke learned from this experience when it test-marketed a new product called C2 for men between the ages of 20 and 40. The C2 product team believed that young men wanted fewer calories but not the taste or image of Diet Coke. Unfortunately the test market revealed that this market segment didn't want a hybrid product that had half the calories of regular Coke. Coca Cola then came back with a winning formula a year later: Coke Zero, which offered the full flavor of Coke with no calories and a new identity.[12]

The process of smart prototyping and pivoting allows a company to validate the market and zero in on the right value proposition. The last step of the innovation process is to design the business model.

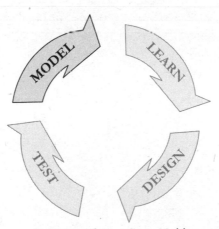

Figure 8.3: The Last Step—Model.

CHAPTER HIGHLIGHTS

- Get early customer feedback to improve your design, get to market earlier with the *right* product, and avoid investing too much money in a colossal failure.
- To get early feedback, show customers a *minimum viable product*—just enough of the new offer to allow customers to offer suggestions.
- Use customer feedback to *pivot* or redesign the new offer or business, until you get it right.

9

NEW WAYS TO MAKE MONEY

THE BOARD PACKAGE

"Thanks for coming by, Bill," said Meena as she offered him a chair in the NaviMark boardroom. "We've got an important board meeting this week and I'd like to run through some of the board package with you."

"No problem at all, Meena," said Bill as he grabbed a seat. "I've been looking forward to seeing what you and your team have been doing since the offsite."

"I think we have a much better plan for growing the business. But it always comes down to the numbers. My board has a limited appetite for visionary ideas."

"I understand. I'll put on my board member hat."

"My plan is to break the presentation into two parts. The first deals with how we put the core business back on a solid growth track. The second part lays out our plan to deliver incremental revenues from our big-data offerings, and how we plan to fund the investment. I'm really excited about the long-term growth strategy we're developing, but I'm not counting on any revenues from new products for the next 18 months."

"Sounds like a sensible approach. Do you still see yourself on an IPO track?"

"*I do,*" *said a determined Meena.* "*It's a slightly longer timetable but I have a much better sense of how we'll get there. The key is in some changes we've made to the business model. I'll start with the P&L over the next 18 months.*"

Meena turned to her laptop and projected the first PowerPoint slide. "*Our Q2 shortfall created a flat spot in our revenue growth and caused us to lose money. Q3 revenue will be slightly better than Q2 but not on the original growth track; on the other hand we'll be back to breakeven profitability. Then, starting in Q4, I'm confident we can get back to 35 percent annual growth with modest profits.*"

"*That's quite a turnaround. How did you get there?*" *said Bill as he scanned through the line items of the income statement.*

"*We made several changes to the business model. First, we cut engineering expenses. Once we concluded that our big-data opportunity would be a longer-term play, we decided not to hire new data scientists and software specialists to build out a new platform. Instead we have a small, dedicated new product team that will be developing and testing prototypes with a handful of customers who are interested in working with us. Thanks to your prodding we stumbled on a couple of very promising applications that are outside of our traditional marketing analytics market. I'll come back to this in part two of the presentation.*"

"*We're going to reinvest some of the engineering expense savings into lead-generation programs. Kemi Ramu has done an amazing job in a short amount of time proving that there are better ways to find qualified customers. The team spent a lot of time looking at where we win and lose deals, and developing a sharper profile of the kinds of companies who can get the most out of our product. We've decided to focus on consumer products and services companies. We know a lot more about the buyer and the limitations of the tools they're using. We've already had a big turnout for a couple of new webinars we developed. And we're starting to cultivate partnerships with other marketing services companies. The results are showing up in our pipeline. I'm ready to bet on scaling up this program.*"

"*That's great news. I'd actually like to see the pipeline numbers,*" *said Bill.*

"I've got a detailed analysis of the pipeline in the marketing section. We're starting to measure pipeline coverage, for example, and we think we'll have 3.5 times our Q4 goal."

"That'll make Anthony's job easier," said Bill. "Do the new marketing programs account for all of the increase in revenue growth?" Bill asked as he squinted at the detailed projections.

"Actually, Anthony won't be with us much longer," said Meena. "We've had some long and challenging conversations. He's not bought into all of the changes we need to make. To be honest, I think he was expecting the sales process to be a lot easier than it turned out to be."

"Wow. That's a big organizational shakeup. How do you think the board will react to Anthony's departure?"

"I've already talked with them," said Meena. "Needless to say, they're uncomfortable with the idea of losing a seasoned executive like Anthony. But I'm the person who needs to deliver the results and I told them that Anthony is the wrong person for the job. It makes the stakes that much higher for me to deliver a strong new plan."

"Good for you, Meena. I hope you can find a good replacement soon. OK, so the additional revenue comes from services?" Bill asked.

"Very perceptive of you. We realized we were missing an opportunity to help our customers install and customize our dashboard for their specific applications. In fact there's an opportunity to create a packaged solution to improve repeat purchases and customer retention. We're not sure we can charge more for the product but we're sure we can sell services. I've tapped several members from engineering and the support group to start a professional services team. They're already testing a few service concepts with some of the customers we met over the last two months. Tina thinks we can ramp services to 15 percent of revenues. I'm also going to begin a search for a VP of Services."

"So you'll need to find a VP of Sales and a VP of Services?"

"I think we have the opportunity to add two talented executives to the team," Meena said without hesitation. "I get lots of inquiries from executives who want to join us, and I think our story is getting better than ever. In the meantime, I can manage the sales team for a few *months; we have strong territory managers. And Patrick is going to help the services team package the new offerings; with Kemi on board he's got more time on his hands."*

"Whew. My head is spinning with all of these changes," said Bill. "But I have to admit that the numbers look really solid. It's all in the execution."

Meena looked calmly at Bill, "Don't worry. We'll execute."

"I'm sure you will," Bill said smiling. "You said there was a part two to the growth strategy?"

"There is, maybe the best part—especially if we can stretch the core business for a while. I know there's a limit to how long we can achieve high growth in the marketing analytics market; it's getting crowded. At some point we need to look to another part of the business for our growth engine."

"What about big-data solutions for marketers?" asked Bill.

"Maybe some day. But the opportunity doesn't look big enough soon enough for our big-data technology. Fortunately, we're capable of tackling more complex problems in other markets right now. Our 'listening' expedition with customers turned up some applications we hadn't thought about."

"Such as . . ."

"Manufacturing automation for starters. We've got two large manufacturing companies willing to be design partners for an application that would improve the performance of robotic assembly operations. We've also got a robotics equipment manufacturer that wants to partner with us to develop and market a solution."

"What's the business model?"

"We're not sure. We could continue our direct selling approach. But we could also become an OEM by allowing robotics companies to sell our software with their equipment. One approach we talked about would be to let Rearden's new robotics customers use our software for free for six months; this would allow them to see the value of our software."

"It sounds like a big investment. Will you be able to breathe life back into your fundraising process?"

"That's the interesting thing. I'm not sure we'll need any financial investors. The two design partners are willing to give us as much as $2 million dollars in the form of prepaid royalties if they can have exclusive use of the software in their industry for a period of time. And the robotics company is interested in making a strategic investment as a way of strengthening the partnership. They're open to any reasonable valuation."

"So you can put off fundraising for awhile."

"Ideally forever," said Meena with a sly grin. "But I don't want to get ahead of myself."

"So your new S-Curve is a big bet on big data and robots?" said Bill.

"Not entirely," said Meena. "I want to make a few small bets until I'm sure we've got a new S-Curve that can move the needle. Actually I was hoping to spend a few minutes with you on the life sciences market. You said you've been consulting for some companies in that industry? . . ."

BUSINESS MODEL DESIGN

With the benefit of prototyping and pivoting there comes a time when a new offer is ready to launch. But before you can launch you need to decide how you will make money. This isn't simply a pricing and sales forecasting exercise. You need to decide on all elements of the business model: pricing, positioning, distribution, partnerships, product delivery process, support, and so on.

When preparing to launch a new S-Curve, don't assume that the new product or service will rely on the same business model you use for your core business. There are many ways to deliver the same offer to a market—some may be wildly successful while others may fall short. In 2008, MySpace and Facebook seemed nearly indistinguishable as leaders in the social media market, each with more than 100 million unique visitors a day. A more careful look would reveal different business models: MySpace was betting on US music lovers, a more free-form style of page design, advertising revenues, and *help* from News Corp, its new owner anxious to generate revenue; meanwhile, Facebook bet on an international audience that loved to share photographs, a simple page design, and a more free-wheeling style of management. Both sides were playing to win the best way they knew how, but only one of these business models succeeded.

Business model design isn't just for new products and services, it's also an important way to drive growth in the core business—stretching the S-Curve—without launching new offers. Who knew that Converse All-Stars would become a fashion shoe? In fact, it's dangerous to think that the business model for your core business can stay the same, as evidenced by the ever-changing home video rental market. The software business provides another stark example.

If Rip Van Winkle were a software CEO who fell asleep in 2003, he wouldn't recognize the business when he woke up 10 years later. As outlined in Figure 9.1, a combination of new technology and business practices has changed almost every aspect of the software business:

So what exactly is a business model? We all know one when we see one, but ask five executives to define a business model and you'll get five different answers. This makes it challenging to have a conversation about tuning the business model. It's not enough to just say that a business model is a way to

Business Model Component	Typical Software Business Model	
	2003	2013
Pricing	Perpetual license	Monthly subscription
First Release	Version 1.0	*Minimum Viable Product*
Capital Investment	Software, hardware	None (cloud computing)
Office Lease	2 to 5 years	None (Incubator space)
Marketing	Trade shows, public relations, seminars	Word-of-mouth, social media, webinars
Sales Model	Direct	Indirect and self-service
Fundraising	$5M venture capital	$0.5M angel investors

Figure 9.1: Evolution of the Software Business Model.

make money. And most executives have a limited repertoire when they need to think about business model alternatives. The disruptive trend that could threaten your brittle business model may be something you can anticipate by learning from other industries.

The subject of business model design can be so diffuse that one strategist named Alexander Osterwalder decided to put a stake in the ground—a starting point for a discussion of business model design. Osterwalder declared that you can describe any business model using nine *building blocks:*

Customer Segments	Value Proposition	Key Partners
Customer Relationships	Key Activities	Revenue Stream
Channels	Key Resources	Cost Structure

To help individuals and teams with the creative process of business model design he organized these building blocks into a *business model canvas* that anyone can download for free,[1] print as a large poster board at the Staples Copy Shop, and tape to a wall for business design working sessions.

It takes a small investment of time to understand these nine elements, but this tool is gaining currency among design-thinking business strategists as a standard way to convey a business model. The business model canvas can help an existing business tune its strategy, allow a new venture (or a new S-Curve) to create its first business model, or help a large company evaluate an acquisition target. Imagine that you were the team at Microsoft behind the acquisition of Skype. You convinced Steve Balmer that Microsoft could earn a return on the $8.5 billion it paid for a company that reportedly had $860 million in revenue and modest losses. Now what? Maybe start with a simple business model canvas of Skype and then sort through ways Microsoft can alter the Skype model to create new value. Can Microsoft find new ways to compete with Google Docs or Citrix GoToMeeting? Can Skype become a standard platform for making Microsoft products more interactive, eliminating architecture debates and creating a time-to-market advantage? One can only imagine.

Thinking about several components of your business model at once can be daunting. It's easier to explore changes to just *one* component at a time, holding all other components constant. To identify alternative options it helps to look outside your industry for some fresh approaches. Look at how Mercedes uses subscription pricing for its jet engines, how Dropbox acquires customers through referrals, how the Apple store delivers a great experience and nearly twice the revenue per square foot of any other retailer. To provide a head start, here is a brief look at five of the most powerful levers of business model design: positioning, customer acquisition, pricing, distribution, and value-added.

POSITIONING

Positioning may be the most valuable component of growth strategy for any company—from the newest startup to a large established business developing a new S-Curve. It's also the hardest to get right. It's the way you let customers know that you have a better solution for their problem—your unique value proposition. Without good positioning, a product with great potential can go unnoticed. The key is to *focus on the problem, not the product.*

Novera Software had a positioning problem. It sold—get ready for this— a Java application server with an LDAP directory and an object-to-relational data mapping utility. Who wouldn't want that? To make things worse, its product had the unremarkable name of EPIC (which stood for "enterprise platform for Internet computing").

Novera didn't know what problem it was trying to solve; it was technology in search of a market. Some of the best engineers in the Boston area had written a million lines of software code but no one seemed to know who the customer was supposed to be. There were already eight application servers on the market—what made EPIC different? Until the company addressed its positioning problem it was unable to raise money, hire new talent, or help the sales team close its best prospects. Fortunately, Novera had managed to win a few customers, and talking to them was the beginning of a process of positioning Novera for success.

Over the next four months Novera's leaders spent time in the field listening to many chief information officers. They learned that large information technology (IT) organizations were struggling with a new problem—how to get a new class of web applications to communicate with their enterprise software applications such as Oracle and SAP. These IT teams had relied on enterprise application integration (EAI) software to connect Oracle to SAP, but EAI software wasn't designed to work with web applications. As it turned out, Novera's engineering team had anticipated this new kind of integration problem—they just never explained this to the rest of the team. Management decided to position the Novera server (no longer EPIC) as a solution to *web* application integration. They used the acronym WAI to describe the company's solution category—like EAI software but with a focus on web applications.

With this one change in positioning, Novera had a dramatic increase in customer interest, analysts started writing about the company, and the team could finally raise money and hire additional executives. Later that year, a publicly traded EAI vendor approached Novera with an attractive acquisition offer. They coveted the WAI story; they wanted to offer an end-to-end integration solution from the Internet to the back office. And the way Novera unlocked this value was to position itself around the problem, not its product.

When your positioning focuses on the product it makes the customer work too hard to find you—why would anyone need a Java application server? Customers must first try to understand your description of your product or service, and then somehow make the connection to a problem they may have. This approach leaves too much to chance. In contrast, when you begin with the problem, you make a direct connection to customers with that problem. They want to learn more even before they know what you're selling. Take this positioning statement from a growth company called Gazelle: "Gazelle pays consumers for used smartphones, and other electronic devices—helping them upgrade faster or put some extra money in their pockets. All while doing some good for the planet by finding homes for the devices they no longer need." You don't know anything about how this service works, but you sure know when to call Gazelle.

Compare these positioning statements, both from leading startups in the big data analytics market:

Positioning around a Product: The BlueKai Data Activation System (DAS) is an enterprise-level, cloud-based platform that manages your data assets and provides a common data management system for all your marketing and customer interaction programs.

Positioning around a Problem: ZestFinance helps lenders in all credit segments better assess the credit risk of potential borrowers.

Which statement do you believe will attract more prospects?

Take a look at your own positioning statement. Are you positioning around your product, or around the problem you solve? Of course, if you're not sure what problem you solve, you may want to spend more time listening to your customers.

CUSTOMER ACQUISITION

Growth companies are constantly searching for more efficient ways to acquire customers. Customer acquisition cost is one of the most important drivers of the profitability of subscription pricing models. The first step, of course, it to measure the effectiveness of various marketing programs and to choose those that generate qualified opportunities at the lowest cost. But there are other ways to amp up customer acquisition at low cost.

One approach is to reward customer referrals. Every time you introduce a new user to Dropbox, the company will award you an additional 500MB of free storage. For a service designed to connect users this incentive has had made an enormous impact on subscriber growth at a minimal cost to Dropbox. Finding a way to drive viral or word-of-mouth marketing takes advantage of the fact that your customers are already connected to other qualified prospects you want to reach.

Another effective customer acquisition approach is inbound marketing, attracting prospects to your company by giving away helpful information and creating communities of prospects with shared interests. Hubspot is a growth company that offers the best online library of resources for marketers in small to medium-sized businesses. You can learn about search engine optimization, running successful webinars, creating successful social media sites, and writing effective e-books by attending their webinars, downloading their e-books, and attending their academy. All of this free advice has helped Hubspot attract over 1 million followers to its blog. It's also helped attract more than 10,000 paying customers for the company's marketing software.

Some companies like Chipotle invest in customer loyalty and the in-store experience rather than advertising campaigns. Evidence of Chipotle's word-of-mouth success is its more than 2 million Facebook fans.

Another creative approach to customer acquisition is *freemium* pricing.

PRICING

Do you use LinkedIn, Skype, or Mint? When it comes to pricing strategy, *free* is the new black. Companies have learned that the best way to attract customers and build loyalty is to initiate the relationship by giving something away free.

Free is not a new marketing concept. In 1900, King Gillette came up with a new way to attract customers to his shaving equipment business: give away the razor and charge for the blades. To recover the cost of free razors, Gillette had to be sure that customers bought only his high-margin blades. Good luck finding a generic blade to fit a Gillette razor; the razor blade is one of the most patented of all consumer products. You'll recognize the *razors and blades* strategy when you get a free printer with your purchase of a computer; the printer company recoups its costs with its high-margin ink cartridges. Another example is your free or highly subsidized smartphone, which is available from wireless service providers as long as you sign up for a two-year service contract.

A more recent twist on *free* is the *freemium* pricing strategy: give away a basic version but charge for a premium version. One of the early adopters of this approach was Netscape when it encouraged individuals to use its new Internet browser for free; businesses, however, had to pay for the premium version. Many Internet-based businesses have followed suit. Skype lets you make free phone and video calls but charges you to call a landline or mobile phone. Dropbox provides enough free storage for most users but charges a monthly fee for storage beyond this basic allotment. The *New York Times* on-line edition lets you read the headlines and 10 stories per month for free; to read more than 10 full-length stories per month you need an online subscription. There's no charge for using LinkedIn to manage your contacts, but if you want to know who's been looking at your profile you'll need the premium version; professional recruiters are happy to pay LinkedIn to use its sophisticated search tools. Companies who use the *freemium* model believe that a segment of customers will find the premium version compelling enough that they'll convert to paying customers—and that the resulting revenue stream will more than cover the cost of the free service.

Another important pricing lever is to shift from outright purchase to pay-per-use pricing. Many customers don't have the capital or the need to make an outright purchase of a vacation home, a software program, or a copy machine. Timesharing, software-as-a-service, and Xerox copy services have filled this void. The benefit for companies who offer pay-per-use or subscription pricing is a better business model: *recurring* revenue. Investors prefer companies whose customers make a steady stream of payments over time to those who collect one upfront payment from each customer.

What could you give away for free as a way to build relationships with new prospects?

DISTRIBUTION

One of the best ways to improve the customer experience is to take the friction out of the buying process. A side benefit is a more efficient distribution strategy that can lower the cost of doing business.

Buy a designer desk and you'll be amazed at how many months it takes to select, order, build, and deliver the desk. Sometimes you can only buy the desk through a licensed designer. There will always be a high end in any market. However, most markets are going through a dizzying process of reinventing distribution to shrink the time it takes to find, purchase, and receive a product or service. The goal is immediate gratification and a great experience.

You can sign up for an amazing number of valuable web and mobile applications with just an e-mail and password: Coursera, Open Table, Kayak,

Hertz, Khan Academy, and Amtrak are just a few. Companies whose signup process is challenging or who ask for much more than a username and password can expect a small turnout. With a limited investment in one-time setup, you can make one-click purchases from the best web and mobile sites with just a password. The Internet is setting a new bar for ease of sign-up and purchase.

Western Union and MoneyGram have long ruled the market for money transfers to friends and family in other countries, typically handling cash transactions at brick-and-mortar outlets. However, a new money transfer service from Xoom is disrupting this market with a cheaper, electronic way for customers to send money overseas from their bank or credit card accounts using a mobile device or a computer. Western Union and MoneyGram are responding but, as in any innovator's dilemma, they face the challenge of cannibalizing their traditional distribution channel.

Internet retailing created a direct-to-customer channel that is bypassing retail stores. Amazon is now the most feared competitor of brick-and-mortar retailers. Who would have thought we'd be buying shoes and auto parts online with little concern about the return process? Business is booming at UPS and the customer experience is outstanding. Amazon, eBay, and Google are already moving into a new frontier: same-day delivery.

For their part, brick-and-mortar retailers are reinventing the store by creating a shopping experience that can't be matched on the Internet. Apple designed a high-touch retail experience staffed by some of the best-trained sales associates of any retail store. The results speak for themselves. Apple's revenue per square foot is nearly twice that of second-place Tiffany & Co., and three times that of third-place lululemon athletica. Expect to see more retail geniuses at their bars.[2]

Turning to the business market, there will always be a direct sales channel but you might not see the sales person as often. In-person sales calls are now limited to *big ticket* sales while lower ticket items are sold over the phone by telesales teams. The best telesales professionals are using web conferencing such as WebEx and GoToMeeting where they can combine live video with presentations to deliver a higher-quality meeting experience. It's a wonder that so many sales reps are still on the road.

For businesses worried about secure communications over the Internet, Ping Identity stores credentials in the cloud, allowing employees and business partners to sign in once from any device and then access any business applications securely.

For most businesses, self-service is the end game. If you can make it easy for customers to find what they want, customize the product or service to fit their needs, and place the order, then the customer and the company are both winners. CVS is teaching its customers to use self-checkout. Apple will let you purchase certain products in their stores without a genius. The Hertz mobile app is so easy to use that you can reserve a car, select car models, and find out what stall your car is parked in . . . all in the time it takes to get off a plane.

Customer design takes self-service to another level. Rather than simply ordering what the company has for sale, the customer can design or customize what they're buying. Lego will let you create your own Lego design, allowing you to package all of the pieces required to build, let's say, a replica of your home. Self-publishing authors, such as *Wool*'s Hugh Howey, can choose from a variety of tools and services offered by Amazon and others: hire freelance editors, design your own book jacket, customize your layout, create an electronic book, set pricing, and track sales.

If you're going to launch a new S-Curve, make sure you take all of the friction out of your distribution process.

VALUE ADDED

Every company chooses not only what market to target but also what role to play in the value chain. An important business model design question is what role to play in the value chain (Figure 9.4) and what role to outsource to others. In making this choice a company needs to consider where the money is, what unique capabilities it has to offer, and whether there are advantages to integrating vertically—that is, controlling several value-added roles.

In the personal computer (PC) industry, Intel and Microsoft became the dominant providers of the industry standard Intel x86 microprocessor, the Windows operating system, and Office applications. They extracted

Figure 9.2: Industry Value Chain. Source: Author.

high margins for these unique components and left the other value-added roles, along with meager margins, to PC original equipment manufacturers (OEMs) like HP and Dell. In contrast, Apple chose a vertical integration strategy for its personal computers and smartphone, controlling most elements of the value chain to ensure a better customer experience and maintain high margins. In particular, Apple led with its design skills to define the user experience, the operating system and product architecture, and the shopping and support experience. Apple maintained high margins not only through pricing but also by outsourcing manufacturing and assembly to low-cost providers using a strict set of quality standards. Apple chose *not* to sell applications to avoid competing with the applications providers that make its platform more valuable.

Sometimes it makes sense to stay focused on the one thing that you're good at. Dolby designs systems for improving sound and video signals. Rather than building its own speakers and headphones, the company has chosen to license its patented algorithms (and logo) to consumer electronics manufacturers further down the value chain. Gore-Tex does the same with its patented fabric design, allowing clothing manufacturers to incorporate this breathable, waterproof fabric into the their weather-resistant clothing—while Gore-Tex collects royalties.

Can your company move into a higher value role in the value chain? Is there an opportunity to outsource low value activities?

• • • •

Before launching a new offer, take a careful look at how you will make money. What are the business model choices that will lead you to the greatest market and financial success? It's a mistake to simply map your current business model onto a new solution. In fact, it may even be time to take a fresh look at the business model for your *core* business.

Many view the launch of a new solution as the finish line. But launching a new product or service is just the beginning of a new cycle of learning in the market. It takes a dedicated effort to fine tune the customer experience, the offer, and the business model until you get it right.

These last four chapters described the four Innovation Power Tools: learn, design, test, and model. These tools provide an essential foundation for any innovation process. However, to ensure that the process can proceed alongside a demanding core business, you need committed leadership.

CHAPTER HIGHLIGHTS

- When preparing to launch a new S-Curve, don't assume the new product or service will rely on the same business model you use for your core business.
- Business model design can also be a way to drive more revenue—both for a new S-Curve and from the core business.
- Challenge your assumptions about each element of the business model, considering innovative approaches from other industries.

10
AIR COVER

THE DAILY HUDDLE

Meena liked what she heard as she interviewed a new VP of Sales candidate over breakfast in the Mandarin Oriental in New York. The Asiate restaurant had a spectacular thirty-fifth-floor view of Central Park.

Just then her Galaxy started buzzing.

"Can you excuse me for a few minutes, Ken?" Meena asked. "That's a reminder for me to call in to our daily huddle. The penalty for being late is severe—you have to sing a song. I just can't imagine doing that here."

"No problem," said the candidate. "I'm enjoying the view."

Meena found a quiet room to dial in to her meeting. The daily huddle was a management ritual that Tim Wiggins established when he was CEO. To promote frequent communication and alignment, executives met for ten minutes every day; if you were out of town you were expected to dial in. To ensure that meetings were punctual, Tim had established 9:37 as the start time. No one sat down during a huddle; the agenda was a series of brief updates from each executive to recognize progress, identify problems, and solicit help from other executives.

As the updates moved from executive to executive it was clear that everyone was feeling the pressure to achieve the company's aggressive turnaround goals. The sales team was doing everything possible to make the quarter; new product releases were barely on track; cash was tight. But with the intense focus on day-to-day operations Meena realized something was missing.

"What's happening with the robotics pilot for Rearden Automation?" Meena asked.

Everyone on the call was quiet. Then Albert responded, "We don't have the resources for that project right now. We're struggling to finish the next release of the Navigator."

"How did we leave things with TSC and Rearden?" asked Meena.

"I'm not sure," said Tim. "I need to check with Tara Phalen, the lead engineer."

Meena thought for a moment. "I know we've got some aggressive goals but I don't want to lose momentum on the robotics prototype. That's our future."

"I just need the team for a few weeks," said Albert.

"That's a long time away from the pilot. Does this mean Tara's no longer driving the customer mapping project we started?"

"She and the robotics team are heads down on the Navigator release, like everyone on the engineering team. It's all hands on deck right now," said Albert.

"I understand what you're saying, Albert. Let's catch up later this afternoon so I can understand some of the tradeoffs you're dealing with in development," said Meena. "I just have one more question. Does anyone have any customer visits planned for this month?"

There was a long pause before Tina Thorn jumped in, "Meena, until we close this quarter on plan the resources will be really tight everywhere. I'm not sure anyone on the team has the luxury of customer visits this month. And I'm trying to keep the travel budget under control."

"I guess we all have a lot going on right now," said Meena, sensing the pressure the entire executive was feeling. "If there are no other topics this morning, let's all get back to work. I'll see you all later this week."

Later in the day, Meena caught up with Albert by phone. "Albert, I'm worried about re-assigning the key people we had on the skunkworks—that *project is really important to our future. Is your development schedule really that tight?*

"I'm sorry, Meena. I meant to talk with you about this. We ran into technical problems that required more engineering staff and we needed Tara to backstop a very junior product manager assigned to this release."

"What would happen if we released these product features a few weeks later than planned?" asked Meena.

"I don't think it would affect revenues, but we'd miss a board commitment."

"I really want Tara and her engineering team to stay focused on the Rearden project. If we need to slip the next release a couple of weeks, I can take the heat for missing the board commitment. Can we find a middle ground and transition Tara and team back to the pilot?"

"Alright, Meena, let me see what I can do. Supporting these new product initiatives while trying to keep the existing business on track is a real balancing act."

"It's a challenge for me as well, Albert. But it's a balancing act that I want us all to master so that we can be successful in the long run. Does that make sense?"

Two days later, Meena was briefing her board member, Micaela San-chez, in preparation for the next board meeting.

". . . So, for the quarter, I expect us to be on plan for our revenue and profits and nearly all of our quarterly goals," said Meena. "The one goal we're going to miss . . . slightly . . . is the release date on the next version of Navigator."

"That's surprising," said Micaela, "I can't remember the last time that Albert missed a delivery date."

"Albert was prepared to meet the original plan, but only by using resources we had dedicated to the Rearden project," said Meena, knowing what was coming.

"The Rearden project?" said Micaela. "Is that so critical right now?"

"If we don't keep that project moving our design partners could start looking at other alternatives."

"I thought that we were just researching different markets. I didn't know we were making this kind of commitment to the robotics market," said Micaela. *"You probably sense that I'm skeptical that this company can make a transition from marketing automation to managing robots. I've never liked company transitions."*

That night, Meena sent a text message to Bill:

free for coffee this week? I might have an opportunity for you . . .

INNOVATION LEADERSHIP

Without strong leadership, innovation will fail. Leaders don't need to come up with the innovations themselves, but they play several critical roles to ensure that innovation can flourish in their organizations. They make clear the company's growth objectives and the role innovation plays in getting there. They create and preserve the kind of culture that makes room for innovation. They provide the *air cover* for fledging projects that would otherwise be shut down or starved for resources. And when it's time to make a decision—go or no-go—they're able to pull the trigger.

Founders hold a special status when it comes to innovation. They have the track record, experience, and company following to rally the organization around the next big bet. They're like the veteran players on a sports team who have the experience of playing in a championship game. Leaders who succeed the original founders have a tough act to follow when it comes to new product innovation; many rely on *design partners*—senior executives who specialize in new product development.

Leading the innovation process is a balancing act for any senior executive. It requires thinking and operating across two different kinds of business models. One, the core business that needs to grow and deliver cash flows to support future investments. The other, a *skunkworks:* a loosely structured environment where small teams operating independently have the freedom to explore radically new ideas. Pursuing each of these initiatives is a virtual, entrepreneurial team trying to work faster and with less structure than the

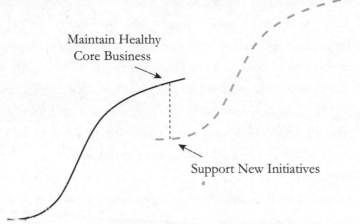

Maintain Healthy
Core Business

Support New Initiatives

Figure 10.1: Business Model Balancing Act.

organization is used to. It's the special role of the leader to keep the core business healthy while ensuring that new initiatives have room to grow.

THE GROWTH IMPERATIVE

We all know that innovation is a good thing; just look at all of the corporations with banners and slogans affirming their commitment to innovation: *Innovation 2020!* But it's not enough to say, "Row faster!" Employees need to understand *why* the company needs to grow, and the role of innovation in achieving these objectives. This is a question the leader must answer.

There are a number of important reasons for a company to embrace growth:

- **Market Leadership:** If the market is growing 30 percent per year and your company is growing 20 percent per year, you're losing market share. Market leaders grow faster than the market—often a lot faster than the market. The advantages of leadership can be compelling; imagine what it's like to be *number two* in Internet search, online book sales, or Greek-style yogurt. Everything gets easier when you're the market leader, though it may be hard to get there in the first place. It's the CEO's job to make sure everyone understands what's at stake when the company is battling for first place.

- **Employee Expectations:** If Workday, the new upstart in cloud-based enterprise applications, or GoDaddy, the domain name company that's been on the Inc. 5000 list since 2004, stopped growing, would the same people still want to work there? To attract and retain a certain caliber of high performers, a company must sustain the kind of growth that funds new investment and creates new career opportunities.
- **Investor Expectations:** If a growth company stops growing, will the same growth-oriented investors want to maintain or increase their ownership—at the same valuations? For companies who have set high expectations with private investors or the stock market, growth is the only way to deliver results.
- **Mission:** Mission-driven companies are not content to be successful in one or two product categories; they're driven to fulfill a mission that transcends any product category. Success with today's products or services provides the brand and resources to continue to pursue the mission with *new* products and services. Consider what it means to pursue some of these missions:
  - Nike: *Bring inspiration and innovation to every athlete in the world.*
  - Google: *Organize the world's information and make it universally accessible and useful.*
  - Vestergaard: *Improve the health of vulnerable people, most of whom live in developing countries.*

Communicating the company's growth objectives is not simply a financial discussion, but an important step to ensure alignment across a growing organization. Busy leaders may believe that the need to grow is obvious; but with less time to spend communicating with more employees, the growth imperative can get fuzzy. The problem is even worse for new employees— nothing is obvious to the uninformed.

Perhaps you've heard the story of the bricklayer and the cathedral. A visitor to a construction project asks a bricklayer what he's doing and the bricklayer responds, "Can't you see that I'm laying bricks?" The visitor asks a second bricklayer the same question but this bricklayer responds with some pride, "I'm building a wall." Finally, the visitor asks a third bricklayer what she's doing. This bricklayer stands and dusts herself off, points her arm up into the air and says, "I'm building a cathedral." We all want to be inspired by the role we can play.

Once an executive team understands its growth target, it needs to take a realistic look at how much of that target it can achieve with existing products and services over a three-year period. This *gap analysis* reveals how much of the company's future revenues must come from *new* products and services. Filling that gap becomes the *innovation challenge*. The size of the gap indicates how aggressive the company must be in pursuing innovation. If the gap is $30 million in three years, then the expected value of the revenue from all innovation activities needs to exceed $30 million.

The size of this gap as a percentage of company revenues varies dramatically depending on the business. Companies with aggressive growth targets in industries with rapid product cycles (e.g., solar panels) may see gaps of

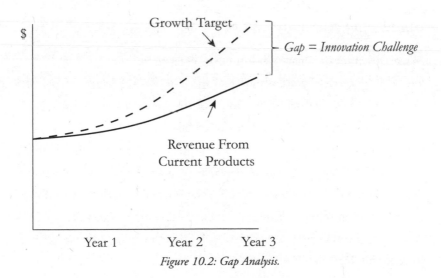

Figure 10.2: Gap Analysis.

50 percent or more in three years. Companies with modest growth targets operating in mature markets (e.g., auto components manufacturers) may have gaps of only 10 to 15 percent of revenues. Most ambitious and realistic growth company executives anticipate a gap of at least 30 percent, and this translates into the need for one or more substantial new offers that do not exist today.

It's possible to fill some of this gap through acquisition. However, acquisition as a growth strategy has its own challenges. It's very hard to find a complementary product or service, one that might serve the same customer and have a similar distribution channel. It's also extremely difficult to integrate a new team into the culture of the acquirer. And it's nearly impossible to make such an acquisition at a reasonable valuation, particularly when it involves two private companies—the owners and investors on both sides always want a better deal. It may be easier to make an acquisition as a public company using publicly traded shares for currency. In any case, acquisition is unreliable as a stand-alone growth strategy; larger companies often hedge their bets by pairing an acquisition strategy with internal innovation initiatives to sustain long-term growth.

Once the growth imperative and the innovation challenge are clear, the leader needs to create an environment that promotes innovation.

INNOVATION CULTURE

What does it mean to have a culture that fosters innovation?

The biggest cultural barriers to innovation are the fears of personal failure and career setback. Dave and Tom Kelley, the founders of IDEO, argue that too many people are insecure about their creative abilities; they often *learn* at an early age that they're failures in creative activities. Only by regaining a degree of *creative confidence* can these individuals see failure as an important way to learn, allowing them to take on the kinds of challenges that lead to breakthroughs.[1] Even those with personal courage may be stymied in an environment where risk taking may be encouraged . . . as long as you don't fail.

Leaders play a pivotal role in setting the tone for risk taking and innovation in their companies. The first step is to look past the promotional hype designed to turn every employee into a creative genius and ask: what happens to teams that fail? If the answer is that these teams disappear into the backwater of the company, or that the project becomes *That-Which-Must-Not-Be-Named*, it sends a chilling signal about the consequences of failure. A better approach is to reward failure.

In 2010, Google launched Wave—a new web application for real-time communication and collaboration. Despite the company's enthusiasm and substantial investment, Wave failed to gain traction. In announcing the shutdown, then CEO Eric Schmidt said publicly: "We celebrate our failures. This is a company where it is absolutely OK to try something that is very hard, have it not be successful, take the learning and apply it to something new."[2] Reinforcing this message for the Wave team, Google Fellow Urs Holzle posted a message on the Google Official Blog, excerpted here: "Wave has taught us a lot, and we are proud of the team for the ways in which they have pushed the boundaries of computer science."[3]

Gray Advertising created the *Heroic Failure* award for a courageous account executive who took a big risk and failed. To win the business from a kitty litter manufacturer, Amanda Zolten tested the product with her own cat—and then hid the used kitty litter under the conference table while she made her pitch. When she revealed her secret—intended to show how well the product masked the odor—she received mixed reactions from the client. But her boss wasted no time in rewarding the effort.[4]

Another way to lead is for the CEOs to go out on a limb with their own stretch goals. Jeff Bezos is using his own money—more than $30 million—to build a clock designed to last 10,000 years. The clock will tick once a year; the century hand will move once every 100 years, and the cuckoo will appear once a millennium. What's the point? Bezos explains on his website: "It's a special Clock . . . an icon for long-term thinking. Humans are now technologically advanced enough that we can create not only extraordinary wonders but also civilization-scale problems. We're likely to need more long-term thinking."[5]

I guess it's safe to take a few risks at Amazon.

EXECUTIVE AIR COVER

Even when companies inspire employees to take risks, there are other obstacles in established businesses: approval processes, the competition for resources, and investor expectations. This is why it's so critical for innovation
projects to have executive air cover.

Innovation initiatives will never be able to compete effectively for resources unless the company leader communicates that certain initiatives are
strategic, their resources are off limits to other departments, and the leader
has a personal interest in the success of these initiatives. Without this kind
of support, any initiative is vulnerable to the white corpuscles of company
bureaucracy. How many signatures does it take to launch a new initiative,
build a prototype or secure more resources? To encourage personal initiative, Google and 3M give engineers up to a day a week to pursue their own
projects without approvals. How much discretionary budget—some call it
mad money—is set aside for innovation projects? Once upon a time there
was an R&D budget for new product development, sometimes as much as
5 percent of revenues; but the R&D budget shouldn't belong to one department anymore.

Perhaps more critical to innovation is setting expectations with investors.
Innovation requires investment with little certainty about returns, something
investors try to avoid. Investors want to see a smooth, predictable increase in
earnings over time. They want to see a direct connection between investment
dollars in and earnings dollars out—all in a *reasonable* time frame. Investment in innovation takes more of a leap of faith; but without the conviction
to pursue innovation, with all of its uncertainties, a company runs the risk of
racing to the end of its current S-Curve with no backup plan. The more risk-
averse the investors are, the more focused they are on returns from the *current*
S-Curve. New S-Curves don't lend themselves to ROI—they're *growth stories.*

If there were a Hall of Fame for *Executive Air Cover,* Jeff Bezos would
have been inducted long ago. Look at the price-to-earnings (P/E) ratio of
Amazon.com and you'll discover something astounding.

Let me first explain what a P/E ratio is, and why it's a useful indicator of
investor expectations for growth. The price-to-earnings ratio—often referred

to as the price-to-expectations ratio—is the price of a stock divided by its annual earnings. The price investors are willing to pay for a stock says a lot about their belief in the company's future growth potential. If a company was earning $1 per share but wasn't expected to grow much, you might be willing to pay $10 per share to earn a 10 percent return but with little prospect for growth; that would equate to a P/E ratio of 10. However, if you thought the company was going to double its earnings per share in three years, you might be willing to pay $20 for the stock today, which would amount to a P/E ratio of 20. P/E ratios of 30 or higher are considered to be at the *nose-bleed* level; if a company whose stock is trading at these levels reports a disappointing quarter, the stock can tumble—not because the company is in trouble but because investors have less confidence in the long-term growth prospects that are built into the stock price and P/E ratio.

If you look at the P/E ratios of some of the most successful growth companies over the period 2010–2013 you'll see the following ranges: Apple 10 to 23; Google 19 to 38, Starbucks 12 to 45. In contrast, Amazon's P/E ratio has remained well over 50 since 2010, was well over 100 during 2012, and *exceeded 3000* for much of 2013.[6] How can this be? Is this the biggest selling opportunity you'll ever see? Before you go shorting the stock, remember that one definition of success is *expectations minus results*. And then look at how Amazon delivers its financial results relative to the expectations that Jeff Bezos established for investors long ago. Amazon has consistently delivered spectacular revenue growth for more than a decade. However, rather than using its market position to deliver similarly spectacular *earnings* growth, Amazon has chosen to invest its cash flows in the business and deliver, well, paltry earnings to shareholders. When you keep the E in the denominator low while you continue to build value, you can drive the P/E ratio pretty high.

Jeff Bezos began managing investor expectations with his "1997 Letter to Shareholders." A few excerpts from this letter make clear his message for Amazon investors:

We first measure ourselves in terms of the metrics most indicative of market leadership: customer and revenue growth, the degree to which customers continue to purchase from us on a repeat basis, and the

strength of our brand . . . we want to share . . . our . . . decision-making
approach so that you, our shareholders, may confirm that it is consis-
tent with your investment philosophy:

- We will continue to make investment decisions in light of long-
  term market leadership considerations rather than short-term
  profitability considerations or short-term Wall Street reactions
  [there, he said it] . . .
- We will make bold rather than timid investment decisions . . .
- We will balance our focus on growth with emphasis on long-term
  profitability. . . . At this stage, we choose to prioritize growth
  because we believe that scale is central to achieve the potential of
  our business model.[7]

Take a look at the most recent Amazon Annual Report and you'll find a
copy of this 1997 Letter to Shareholders right behind the current year Letter
to Shareholders. Bezos doesn't want investors to forget. Later, in his 2006 letter to shareholders, Bezos clarified that by *long run* he may be talking about
seven years: "Planting seeds that will grow into meaningful new businesses
takes some discipline, a bit of patience, and a nurturing culture. . . . In our
experience, if a new business enjoys runaway success, it can only *begin* to be
meaningful to the overall company economics in something like *three to seven
years* [emphasis added]."[8]

PULLING THE TRIGGER

There comes a time in every innovation initiative to make a go or no-go decision. In a world of limited resources and imperfect information, companies
need to make big bets without having all of the data . . . they also need to
know when to pull the plug.

Imprivata built a successful business selling an information security solution that allowed users to log in once and then access all of their applications.
As this *single sign-on* market began to mature, CEO Omar Hussain began
searching for other ways to grow the business. His sales results revealed that
he had a major presence in the health care market—60 percent of his sales

were to hospitals. Hussain rallied his team to make a big bet on the health care market, pivoting the company from being an information security generalist serving all industries to becoming a specialist in the health care industry. The ability to help doctors access health care records is more than a security issue—it's a productivity issue. Every mouse click that Imprivata eliminates improves the productivity of doctors and saves hospitals money. Imprivata's new mission is to *enhance care delivery by providing fast, secure access to patient information.* By moving quickly, Imprivata repositioned itself as a leader in a large, growing market.[9]

Netflix CEO Reed Hastings had hoped to make *go* decisions but then things changed. For several years, a large development team secretly worked on Project Griffin, a small set-top box designed to stream movies over the Internet directly to TV sets in the home. It was an ambitious strategy to create a new digital distribution channel; it would disrupt Netflix's existing business model of delivering DVDs by mail. However, within weeks of launching what would have become The Netflix Player, Hastings made the lonely decision to cancel the launch and spin the Player out into a separate company. He realized that by getting into the set-top box business Netflix would be competing with important channel partners for its content business: manufacturers of Blu-ray players, Internet-connected TVs, video game boxes, Apple TV, and others. In retrospect it was the right decision for the company, but it was a *no-go* decision that only a leader with vision could make.[10]

FOUNDERS AS LEADERS

Blackberry never had a chance. Neither did Motorola, Nokia, MySpace, Yoplait, or Barnes & Noble. All of these corporations faced the most dangerous of competitors—the founder-led company. Founders such as Steve Jobs, Jeff Bezos, Howard Shultz, Mark Zuckerberg, and Richard Branson have a natural advantage leading the innovation process. They have the experience, the fearlessness, and the following to coalesce their teams and investors around big bets in a way that established companies with professional managers have a hard time matching.

- Once Steve Jobs decided to sell a phone, the clock was ticking for Motorola, Nokia, and Blackberry. And only Jobs could have convinced the Apple board to get into retail stores, a decision that triggered the resignation of Apple's chairman.[11]
- It took Howard Shultz, in a return to the CEO role in 2008, to put Starbucks back on track. Before he was done with this painful course correction he closed 800 stores, reduced the workforce by 4,000 employees and spent $30 million to fly 10,000 store managers to New Orleans for training. Only a founder could have held the company together during this transition.[12]
- Mark Zuckerberg decided that Instagram was strategic to Facebook's future, a company he did not want his competitors to acquire. And so he bought this emerging mobile photo company—with 17 people and no revenue—for $1 billion with little internal debate. Time will tell how strategic Instagram will be but only a founder could make this kind of a decision.
- Richard Branson, founder of the Virgin Group of over 400 companies, is funding a new business called Virgin Galactic that will allow tourists to travel in space. Anyone want to bet against him?

Founders preserve the small-company culture as long as possible, while hired executives bring company-building experience that the early stage team may lack. But the transition to professional management can threaten a culture of innovation. Professional managers have more pressure to deliver short-term financial results and often lack the credibility to make pivotal strategic changes.

It's not to say that CEOs who were not founders cannot lead the innovation process, but they need to earn their stripes. Marissa Mayer has gotten a lot of running room from her board for an acquisition shopping spree to turn Yahoo around. Her acquisition of Tumblr for $1.1 billion is at least as bold as Mark Zuckerberg's purchase of Instagram (and his subsequent attempt to buy Snapchat for $3 billion). She also eliminated a cherished work-at-home program in an effort to get teams innovating side-by-side in Yahoo's offices. But new executives have a *honeymoon period* to prove their abilities as chief innovation officers. Apple's current CEO, Tim Cook, may know more about the operation of a consumer electronics giant than any other executive; but when it comes to new product innovation he's still establishing his credentials.

What approach can leaders who are not founders take to establish themselves as innovators? Many start by spending a lot of time with customers. Meg Whitman took this approach as the new CEO of Hewlett Packard, logging some 305 one-on-one meetings with customers or partners as well as another 42 roundtable chats with small groups in a one-year period.[13] When it comes to strategy and innovation, the voice of the customer trumps *opinions* about products and technology.

Other executives are turning to senior *design partners* to help lead the innovation effort. *Fast Company* calls them *Dynamic Duos*—the partnerships between CEOs and senior design professionals who are responsible for innovation and customer experience. We've all known that Steve Jobs leaned on Jonathan Ive, an industrial designer that Jobs recruited to build the company's unique design organization. And it's no surprise that the CEO of Nike has a VP of Global Design, the CEO of Twitter has a Creative Director, and the CEO of Jawbone has a Chief Creative Officer. But when Pepsi's CEO has a Chief Design Officer, and McDonalds has a Senior Director of Experience Design Innovation, you can see that this idea is going mainstream.

· · · ·

Leadership is an essential ingredient of innovation, but leadership alone is not enough to sustain growth. To prevent the search for the next S-Curve from moving to the back burner, an organization needs an innovation rhythm—a regularly scheduled forum to ensure alignment across innovation teams and executive sponsors.

CHAPTER HIGHLIGHTS

- Without strong leadership, innovation will fail.
- Leaders need to define the company's growth objectives and the revenue gap that new products and services need to address.

- Leaders do three things well to foster innovation:
  1. Build a culture that encourages risk-taking while rewarding failure;
  2. Provide air cover for innovation initiatives; and
  3. Pull the trigger when it's time for a go or no-go decision.
- Founders have natural advantages when leading the innovation process; leaders who were not founders often partner with senior design executives to help drive the innovation process.

11

INNOVATION IS NOT
A FIRE DRILL

THE DESIGN GROUP

*"Bill, your design group is growing like crazy," said Meena, impressed
by the work of her new Chief Innovation Officer. Meena had persuaded
Bill Kruse to join the company and lead the search for the next S-Curve.
"Look at this modern work space; you recruit a couple of our product
experts, hire a Director of Design and the next thing I know you've got
all of these projects going."*

*"You wanted NaviMark to have an innovation rhythm, and that's
what we're trying to create," said Bill. "Anton was a great hire; Navi-
Mark has never had a designer on its staff. Among other things, he found
this design studio; it's cheaper than getting more office space and we're
only a few blocks away from your building. Our upstairs neighbor is
an incubator with a bunch of big-data startups; we learn a lot just by
hanging around here."*

*"But you seem like you're having too much fun. I can't let the board
see this place," Meena laughed as she pulled out her Black and Red note-
book. "Alright, take me through this rhythm you've been talking about."*

*"The big idea is that we're tracking all of our project ideas through
the four Innovation Power Tools: learn, design, test, and model. Anton*

manages the learn stage; we have a number of NaviMark managers out talking with customers and then participating in our monthly Customer Mapping Meetings. We've dedicated a conference room for these meetings so that we can leave our customer maps on the wall—as a kind of work-in-progress. The meetings take place on the second Friday of every month from 12 to 2. Anton serves Regina's Pizza and Mike's Pastries, so attendance is good. Listening to our customer base is going be a continuous process at NaviMark; we're getting a good cross section of company managers involved in the process."

"How's it going so far?" asked Meena.

"We've only had two sessions, but in both of them it was hard to get a word in edgewise," said Bill. "Once people get over the hurdle of actually scheduling these meetings and interviewing customers, they develop strong opinions about steps we can take to improve the customer experience. We've got a sign in the room inspired by one of Stephen Covey's Seven Habits: 'Begin With The End In Mind.'[1] What we say is: 'Begin With The Customer Experience In Mind.' I'll take you to the customer mapping room when we're done."

"I was wondering when I'd get invited," said Meena, feigning a slight. "How do you turn these customer insights into new product ideas?"

"Once a quarter Anton will be holding half-day design challenges. The idea is to get some cross-functional teams together to help translate customer needs into new solution ideas. We're inviting product managers, engineers, service managers, and anyone else who wants to participate. We've got a wall of fame *to recognize the best design work. We're holding the first one in two weeks."*

"You serving lobster for that one?" Meena whined.

"Soft tacos from Temazcal Cantina."

"Oh my gosh. I'll pretend I didn't hear that."

"I don't have many people so I need to find ways to create virtual innovation teams—which is what we want anyway. Finding the next S-Curve has to be everyone's job."

"What's in the other room?"

"That's our prototyping room. You remember Tara Phelan from the engineering team? She joined the design team to manage our prototyping work. She's hoping to hire an informatics graduate student from your alma mater. She's also cultivating partnerships with our Innovation District neighbor EnerNOC for our energy management projects, and the Broad Institute in Kendall Square for our life sciences projects. The robotics project is still based in Worcester. All of this is a horse race—I can't tell you which of these is going to become our next S-Curve."

"How about the part about launching new products and making money?" asked Meena.

"That's my job. You can see some of my business model canvases on the wall. I'm looking for a local business school intern to help me with these."

"My innovation dashboard is on this other wall. I'm showing all of our active projects as they work their way through the learn, design, test, and model stages. We use green, yellow, and red dots to indicate which projects are moving forward and which ones are stuck."

"This looks really good, Bill. I'd like to have you take a half day of our quarterly offsite to walk everyone through this. I don't want the innovation process to be an island. Will you be ready?"

"Absolutely," said Bill. "I think we're sitting on a gold mine. I'm getting a lot of inbound opportunities now that people know what we're doing. The challenge is going to be saying no to most of these opportunities so we can focus on a few of the right projects."

"I'm glad to hear you're thinking that way. I'd also like you to brief the board at our next meeting."

"I'll be ready," said Bill. "By the way, do you hear much from Massive these days?"

"Almost every week," said Meena. "They want to acquire us, invest in us, partner with us, or do anything they can to stay close. I think we'll find a way to work with them. But frankly, I like being an independent company. This is just starting to get fun."

"How about the fundraising process?"

"Right now we don't need any capital," said Meena. "I wouldn't rule out raising some growth capital to scale up the core business or to fund whatever your new S-Curve turns out to be. But for now I just keep interested investors updated on our momentum. It's a funny thing—everyone seems desperate to give you money just when you need it the least."

"And the IPO?"

"The bankers seem more determined than ever to take us out. But the board is a little more relaxed about the timing. The more we scale the business and prove our ability to grow, the more valuable we become. I also think they'd like us to make more progress on our big data opportunity; it gives more juice to the growth story."

"Which has the added benefit of being true," Bill chimed in quickly. "You ready for a coffee break?"

"Perfect timing," Meena responded.

"Let's head over to Flour. I want to check out their pastry innovations."

INNOVATION RHYTHM

How can you make sure that the next S-Curve will be there when you need it? This is an important question since you can never know for sure when you'll need the next S-Curve, nor can you know how long it will take to discover and launch it. There's one thing you can be sure of though; *if you wait until you're desperate for a new source of growth, it may be too late to do anything about it.* Innovation takes time—it can't be a fire drill.

At the same time, innovation cannot be reduced to a recipe or an assembly line process. The work of learning from customers, designing new approaches, testing new offers, and determining the best way to make money requires a blend of design thinking and decision thinking, experimenting and pivoting. It involves participants from different departments operating as a virtual team with no dedicated budget. Results are difficult to predict. There are no well-established practices for managing this process comparable to those used for business planning or operations management. In fact, too much structure could get in the way. Then what should you look for in an innovation process?

A good innovation process should:

- Be driven by the company's three-year vision and revenue gap;
- Track multiple innovation initiatives, each at different stages of development;
- Evaluate progress, identify obstacles, and make mid-course corrections;
- Reallocate resources to double down on the projects with traction and to stop those that no longer look promising;
- Create alignment on objectives, priorities, actions, and owners.

One way to guide innovation initiatives is to create a process that mirrors the quarterly operating reviews that businesses use to keep the core business—the current S-Curve—on track. These routine executive team meetings create a rhythm for managing operations. An effective innovation process could adopt some of the best features of the quarterly operating review, becoming a parallel process for using the Innovation Power Tools.

Before outlining what an innovation rhythm might look like, it's helpful to understand the best practices in quarterly *operating* reviews as a baseline.

OPERATING RHYTHM

A growth company is like a high-performance sports car—it can deliver great results but it needs frequent tuning and alignment. The best-managed growth companies hold quarterly executive meetings to review company progress and make mid-course corrections. The purpose of these meetings is:

- To track quarterly progress toward the annual operating plan;
- To identify obstacles to achieving the company's objectives—often referred to as "rocks";
- To uncover new opportunities—ways to stretch the S-Curve—that may require additional resources;

- To decide on priorities—what are the three to five most important rocks to move aside or new opportunities to pursue; and
- To create an action plan for each of the priorities including: *who* (the personal accountable), *what* (the deliverable) and *when* (the deadline).

Companies that make these quarterly meetings a part of their routine not only solve problems and anticipate opportunities more quickly, but they also realize a valuable byproduct: alignment of the executive team. Most companies would be better off with complete alignment around an imperfect strategy than to have the perfect strategy without alignment. In fact most teams don't realized how far out of alignment they are; in a recent survey by *Inc. Magazine,* 64 percent of growth company executives said they were in alignment, yet the evidence—the ability of these teams to name the same top three priorities—indicated that only 2 percent of these teams were truly aligned.[2] *Mastering the Rockefeller Habits* has become the bible for growth-stage companies implementing a rhythm of quarterly operating meetings—often followed up with monthly and weekly meetings and daily huddles.

Two quarterly meetings each year have a special purpose. The management offsite in the fourth quarter is dedicated to finalizing the operating plan for the coming year. This is the time when the executive team locks down its financial commitments, priorities, and annual budget. The fourth quarter offsite is necessarily very tactical with a focus on the next 12 months. In contrast, many executive teams reserve the second quarter offsite for a longer-term review of the business: a chance to reflect on the health and future direction of the business over the next three years. The second quarter offsite is usually at least a two-day retreat that allows time to update company goals, evaluate new market opportunities, and prioritize strategic investments. The key agenda item is to update the three-year vision; in fact it's best to start with this topic so that tactical issues don't hijack the agenda.

Three years is an ideal planning horizon for a company vision. Five-year plans are no longer believable; the world moves too fast. And even if employees believed a five-year vision, it's so far in the future that it doesn't inspire action today. Three years is far enough into the future to motivate executives

1st Quarter	2nd Quarter	3rd Quarter	4th Quarter
One-Day Review	**Two-Day Retreat:** *Three-Year Vision*	One-Day Review	Annual Operating Plan

Figure 11.1: Annual Operating Rhythm.

to think expansively about the possibilities for their business, leaving behind today's operational problems. But three years is also near enough that once an executive team gets aligned around a common vision, there doesn't seem to be a minute to lose to lay the groundwork for getting there. The important thing is to make the vision as specific and vivid as possible.

A powerful exercise for the second quarter offsite is for an executive team to work in small groups (four to six participants) to describe or create a picture of the business as they see it in three years. The framework in Figure 11.2 can be a helpful starting point. Participants are asked to describe specific attributes of the business as it will exist in the future. These would include future customers served, revenues and profitability, any changes to the company positioning, new products or services offered, new markets or market

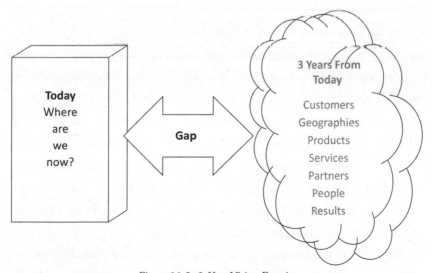

Figure 11.2: 3-Year Vision Exercise.

segments served, geographic expansion, new strategic partners, and any other material changes to the business model and organization. Thinking through the three-year vision at this level of detail allows executive teams to determine whether they're on the same page, and to communicate a common vision to the rest of the organization. It also provides clarity on exactly what the company needs to do to achieve its three-year goals. Chip and Dan Heath describe a similar exercise called the *destination postcard*—a picture postcard from the future that illustrates what is possible.[3]

One important byproduct of the three-year vision exercise is to identify the revenue gap that must be filled by new products and services. Participants estimate how much of year-three revenue will come from existing offers and how much must come from new offers. This gap becomes the company's innovation challenge, as described in chapter 10. The exercise can also kick-start the innovation process by suggesting new high-potential markets and customer needs for the company to explore.

QUARTERLY INNOVATION REVIEWS

Most companies would be hard pressed to describe an innovation process at their company. So how can a company track the important work of innovation without relying on the inspiration of lone geniuses? An ideal approach is to hold *quarterly innovation reviews,* similar to the quarterly operating reviews but dedicated to innovation initiatives—an innovation rhythm to complement a company's operating rhythm.

Attendees at the quarterly innovation review should include executive sponsors, if not the entire executive team, plus project leaders and team members from the various innovation initiatives. The agenda is a review of each initiative using the framework of the four Innovation Power Tools: Have we learned enough from customers to find a good problem to solve? Where are we in the design process? How will we test our ideas? How well do we understand the business model? Figure 11.3 illustrates a sample dashboard to track progress.

For senior executives, the quarterly innovation review can become an opportunity to address several important questions: Are we making enough

	Learn	Design	Test	Model
Initiative #1	Complete →	Complete →	Complete →	Q3
Initiative #2	Complete →	Complete →	Q3	
Initiative #3	Complete →	In Progress	Q4	
Initiative #4	Q3	Q4?		

Figure 11.3: Innovation Process Dashboard.

big bets to close the three-year revenue gap? Are we providing sufficient resources to each initiative? Do we have the right team members involved? Based on what we've learned, should we stop or defer work on any of these initiatives?

The quarterly innovation review can be scheduled during the same week as the quarterly operating reviews—to take advantage of the fact that the executive team is already together—as long as these meetings are held *separately* since their objectives, thinking processes, and time horizons are very different.

	1st Quarter	2nd Quarter	3rd Quarter	4th Quarter
Core Business	One-Day Review	**Two-Day Retreat:** *Three-Year Vision*	One-Day Review	Annual Operating Plan
Innovation Initiatives	Half-Day Review	**One Day Retreat:** *Portfolio Review*	Half-Day Review	Innovation Budget

Figure 11.4: Annual Operating and Innovation Rhythm.

INNOVATION TEAMS

What's the best way to organize the search for the next S-Curve? There are several options. Since every organizational model is a compromise, here are the pros and cons of the three most common structures.

R&D DEPARTMENT: Many companies have dedicated research and development teams whose job it is to develop future products for the company. The advantage of the R&D team is its ability to focus solely on new initiatives. The problem with this structure is that R&D teams are often isolated from the market and from the rest of the organization. As a result product ideas often lack customer input and a sense of market timing. It can also be challenging to hand off a new product to the mainstream organization for commercialization; unless they've been involved in the design process, the engineering, sales, and marketing organizations may fumble the handoff.

PRODUCT MANAGEMENT TEAM: Another conventional approach to developing new products and services is to assign the job to a product manager. The problem is that product managers rarely have enough time to drive *new* product initiatives. Most product managers are fully engaged, if not under water, supporting the current products of the core business. And the demands of the business—meeting sales targets and delivering new product releases on time—often leave product managers with little discretionary time for customer research and new initiatives.

Furthermore, with this traditional model, product managers need engineering and other resources to design a new solution and build prototypes. The innovation initiative can become starved for resources when the next product release for the core business falls behind schedule.

VIRTUAL TEAM: For most companies, the best approach is to create virtual *innovation teams*. These teams are composed of a mix of product managers, engineers, designers, and customer support specialists. They operate under the sponsorship of a senior executive such as the CTO, Chief Product Officer, or VP of Marketing. They often have their own work space. By drawing on members of different functional groups, the innovation initiative stays tethered to the core business; and when the new offer is ready to commercialize, these team members can move back to their functions to ensure the success of the launch.

. . . .

The most important member of any innovation team is the team leader. This role requires an individual who has a deep sense of the customer, is passionate about the new offer, can build a strong cohesive team, communicates the product vision to different constituencies, and can make tough decisions. Leading an innovation initiative might be the most exciting and important job in the company. It's also a great path to becoming a growth company leader.

CHAPTER HIGHLIGHTS

- A critical event in a company's annual planning cycle is to create or update the three-year vision of the business—this exercise helps to define the innovation challenge.
- The innovation process needs its own planning rhythm, similar to a company's quarterly operating reviews.
- A quarterly innovation review can track the progress of each new growth initiative through the four stages of innovation, identify obstacles, and reallocate resources.
- The virtual innovation team is an ideal structure for driving new initiatives, providing a degree of independence while remaining tethered to the core business. Assigning high potential managers to lead innovation teams is also a great way to groom future growth company leaders.

12

JUST THE BEGINNING

LOOKING BACK

"Welcome to our New Employee Boot Camp," said Meena as she addressed the group assembled in the Customer Training Room. "It's important for everyone at Nouvista to understand who we are, how we got here, and where we're going."

"Just a few years ago we were a small private company called Navi-Mark, helping marketing executives to manage their customer acquisition programs. We were so focused on selling one product that we almost lost our way. We had an unpredictable sales process, we weren't helping our customers become successful, and we didn't think beyond the next twelve months. That was when we started listening to our customers and learning more about the many business problems we could help them solve. Our mission today is so much broader that we decided to change our name from NaviMark, which was all about helping marketing professionals, to our current name, Nouvista. Today we help customers see what matters in their business by sifting through oceans of data.

"I brought just two slides with me to show you how we're growing the company. We're investing in several lines of business that you can think of as S-Curves. To make sure we never slow down we're always searching for the next S-Curve. At Nouvista, innovation is part of everyone's job—so we'll be looking forward to your own ideas.

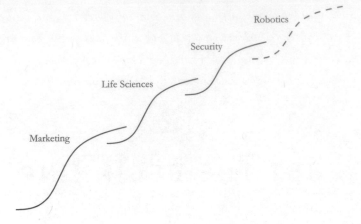

"Today you'll be meeting several members of the executive team. Patrick Howard is the general manager for our traditional products and services for marketing professionals. Bill Kruse leads our life sciences business, which is just exploding right now. And our founder, Tim Wiggins, leads our homeland security business; I might mention that

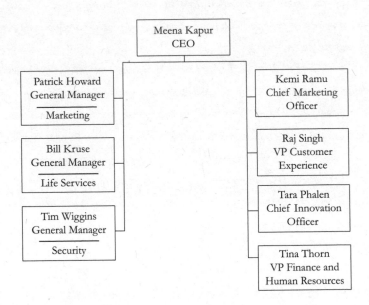

Tim was just named by the Mayor of Boston to the Connected City Task Force. You'll also meet Albert Li who is leading an innovation team that hopes to build a business serving the robotics market."

"I'm hoping that some of you will be leading other new businesses like these in the future. There's no limit to our growth potential as long

as we stay close to our customers, help them solve problems and deliver a great experience." Meena paused to look at the faces in the room and reflected on just how far the company had come—she felt a sense of clarity, such a difference from a few years ago. "Now let me turn things back over to Tina to get the Boot Camp underway."

THE PATH TO UNLIMITED GROWTH

Every organization can aspire to unlimited growth. Only by committing to such a goal—what Jim Collins would call a big hairy audacious goal, or *BHAG*—can leaders hope to achieve it. *The Curve Ahead* outlines a path for getting there. Here's a brief review:

Chapter 1. Every business model matures, following the familiar S-Curve.

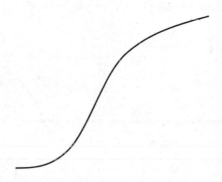

Chapter 2. You can and must *stretch* the S-Curve, but that won't sustain growth forever.

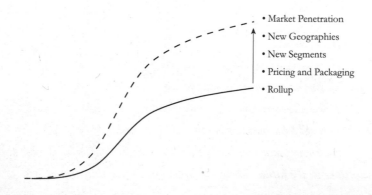

- Market Penetration
- New Geographies
- New Segments
- Pricing and Packaging
- Rollup

Chapter 3. A pipeline management system helps manage the process for stretching the curve and provides an early warning system for business maturity.

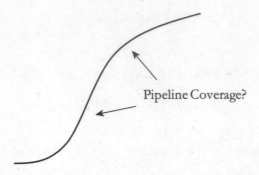

Pipeline Coverage?

Chapter 4. To sustain growth over time you need to find the *next* S-Curve.

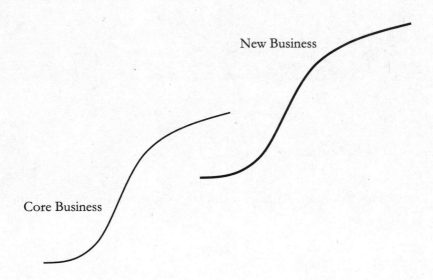

New Business

Core Business

Chapter 5. Finding the next S-Curve, with some predictability, requires an innovation process that incorporates the four Innovation Power Tools: learn → design → test → model.

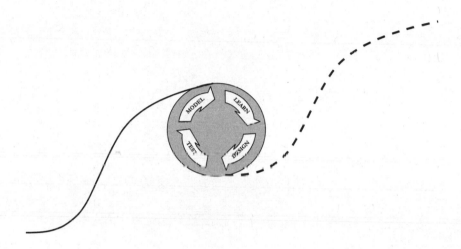

Chapter 6. The first step is to *learn* enough about your customer to stand in their shoes and uncover problems and opportunities that might become new offers. The key is to spend more time with customers, and to listen and observe with empathy.

Chapter 7. Innovation leaders combine design thinking with traditional problem-solving approaches to create breakthrough products and services. First, define an outstanding customer experience, then work backward to *design* the product or service that can deliver that experience.

Chapter 8. Successful innovators *test* their designs early and often with target customers. They know that failure is a part of the roadmap to success, and that frequent trial and error is the way to manage this risk.

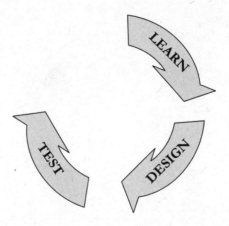

These companies adopt a *lean* approach to testing their designs by creating a simple prototype or *minimum viable product* to solicit customer feedback. They then *pivot* by keeping the parts of the design that resonate with customers, and redesigning the parts that fall short. This iterative process continues until the company gets the customer experience right.

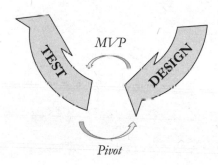

Chapter 9. For new products and services, the ideal business model—the best way to make money—may be very different from the current business model. Innovation in business model design is an essential final step before launch.

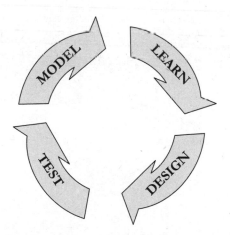

Chapter 10. Driving innovation while growing the core business is a leadership challenge. Leaders need to define the company's future direction, providing clarity on growth objectives and defining the innovation challenge—the gap between the three-year revenue goal and the revenues expected from product and service innovations.

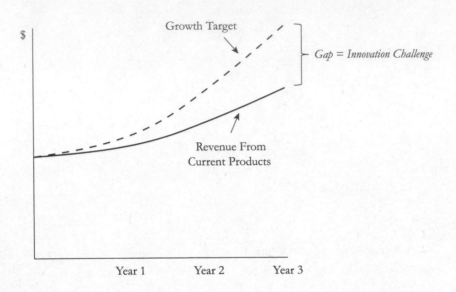

Chapter 11. The innovation process needs its own rhythm—a regular set of meetings to track progress on new innovation initiatives similar to the quarterly process for managing core business operations.

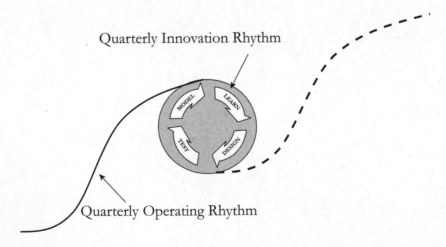

The agenda for the quarterly innovation review is to review the progress of virtual teams driving new initiatives with each of the Innovation Power Tools.

	Learn	Design	Test	Model
New Initiative #1	⟶			
New Initiative #2	⟶			
New Initiative #3	⟶			

NOTES

INTRODUCTION

1. Aeris Partners proprietary research; software industry acquisitions, 2009 to 2013; Shea and Company proprietary research; software industry acquisitions, 2007 to 2010.
2. GE Capital, Ohio State University Fisher College of Business, "The Markets That Move America: GE Capital 2011 National Middle Market Summit" (Ohio: Author, 2011), http://www.middlemarketcenter.org/stuff/contentmgr/files/0/5a30759c139 d09a882c7083f0f00d299/download/the_market_that_moves_america_white _paper.pdf; "About the Middle Market Center," National Center for the Middle Market, http://www.middlemarketcenter.org/about-the-middle-market-center (accessed January 27, 2014).
3. Professor Ashwin Malshe, ESSEC Business School, "The European Mid-Market in 2013," GE Capital, http://www.gecapital.eu/en/docs/LFTM_the_European_mid -market in 2013.pdf.
4. Dr. Rangamohan Eunni, "SMEs in Emerging Markets—An Overview," *International Journal of Emerging Markets*, 2007, http://www.emeraldinsight.com/journals .htm?articleid=1601017&show=html (accessed November 15, 2013).
5. Kauffman Foundation, *High Growth Firms and the Future of the American Economy* (Missouri: Author, 2010), http://www.kauffman.org/what-we-do/research/firm -formation-and-growth-series/highgrowth-firms-and-the-future-of-the-american -economy (accessed September 19, 2013).
6. "Definition and Explanation of 'Gazelle' Company," Investopedia, http://www .investopedia.com/terms/g/gazellecompany.asp (accessed September 19, 2013).
7. "Facts & Figures of the Inc. 5000," *Inc.*, http://www.inc.com/inc5000/2013/facts -and-figures.html (accessed September 19, 2013).

CHAPTER 1: WHY GROWTH COMPANIES STOP GROWING

1. Associated Press, "LoJack Hoping to Give High Tech Heads-Up on Auto Theft," *USA Today*, October 2, 2002, http://usatoday30.usatoday.com/tech/news/tech innovations/2002-10-02-car-theft_x.htm (accessed September 19, 2013).
2. Brian Hindo, "LoJack's Stronger Signal," *Businessweek*, January 15, 2006, http:// www.businessweek.com/stories/2006-01-15/lojacks-stronger-signal (accessed September 20, 2013).

3. "The 200 Best Small Companies," *Forbes,* October 8, 2008, http://www.forbes.com /lists/2008/23/biz_200smalls08_LoJack_4HGA.html (accessed September 19, 2013).

4. Telis Demos, "LoJack Stock is a Steal," *CNN Money,* October 9, 2006, http://money .cnn.com/2006/08/22/smbusiness/lojack.fortune/ (accessed September 20, 2013).

5. Leah Goldman and Alyson Shontell, "Groupon's Billion Dollar Pivot: The Incredible Story of How Utter Failure Morphed into Fortunes," *Business Insider,* March 4, 2011, http://www.businessinsider.com/groupon-pivot-2011-3?op=1 (accessed September 20, 2013).

6. Tara Lachapelle, "Google Would Be Nuts to Buy Groupon, Even at a Huge Discount," *Business Insider,* December 11, 2012, http://www.businessinsider.com/google -would-be-nuts-to-buy-groupon-even-at-a-huge-discount-2012-12 (accessed September 20, 2013).

CHAPTER 2: HOW FAR CAN YOU STRETCH?

1. "Inc 500 Company Profile: Chobani," *Inc,* August 2012, http://www.inc.com /profile/chobani (accessed January 28, 2014); Sheridan Prasso, "Chobani: The Unlikely King of Yogurt," *Fortune,* December 12, 2011, http://money.cnn.com/2011/11 /29/smallbusiness/chobani_yogurt_hamdi_ulukaya.fortune/ (accessed January 27, 2014); Michael Hill, "Greek Yogurt on a Marathon-like Growth Spurt," *USA Today,* January 27, 2012, http://usatoday30.usatoday.com/money/industries/food /story/2012-01-28/greek-yogurt-boom/52826382/1 (accessed January 28, 2014); Sarah Needleman, "Old Factory, Snap Decision Spawn Greek-Yogurt Craze," *Wall Street Journal,* June 20, 2012, http://online.wsj.com/news/articles/SB1000142405 2702303379204577476974123310582 (accessed January 27, 2014); Elaine Watson, "The Rise of Greek Yogurt," *Food,* April 9, 2013, http://www.foodnavigator -usa.com/Markets/The-rise-and-rise-of-Greek-yogurt.-But-is-the-growth-sustainable (accessed January 27, 2014); Morgan Korn, "Greek Yogurt Takes America By Storm," *Yahoo,* August 30, 2012, http://finance.yahoo.com/blogs/daily-ticker /greek-yogurt-takes-america-storm-185609108.html (access January 27, 2014); David Palmer, "The Rise of Greek," *UBS Investment Research,* March 22, 2011, p. 5; E.J. Schultz, *"Who's Winning the Greek Yogurt Revolution," Ad Age,* June 6, 2012, http:// adage.com/article/cmo-strategy/winning-greek-yogurt-revolution/235206/ (accessed January 27, 2014); Mamta Badkar, *"Trendy Greek Yogurt Chobani Is Officially the Top Selling Brand in America," Business Insider,* October 8, 2011, http://www .businessinsider.com/americas-favorite-yogurt-2011-10 (accessed January 27, 2014).

2. Elaine Watson, "The Rise and Rise of Greek Yogurt: But Is the Growth Sustainable?," *Food Navigator-USA,* April 9, 2013, http://www.foodnavigator-usa .com/Markets/The-rise-and-rise-of-Greek-yogurt.-But-is-the-growth-sustainable (accessed September 26, 2013).

3. Chobani Inc., *Chobani Media Kit 2013,* http://chobani.com/who-we-are/resource -lib/ (accessed October 1, 2013).

4. Sheridan Prasso, "Chobani: The Unlikely King of Yogurt," *CNN Money,* November 30, 2011, http://money.cnn.com/2011/11/29/smallbusiness/chobani_yogurt _hamdi_ulukaya.fortune/index.htm (accessed September 26, 2013).

5. David Prasso, "The Rise of Greek Yogurt," UBS Investment Research, March 22, 2011, p. 4.

6. "The Inc. 5,000 List 2013," *Inc.,* http://www.inc.com/inc5000/list (accessed October 6, 2013).

7. Burt Helm, "The Sandwich that Ate the World," *Inc.,* April 30, 2013, http://www .inc.com/magazine/201305/burt-helm/how-i-did-it-fred-deluca-subway.html (accessed October 2, 2013).

8. Ibid.

9. Emily Maltby, "Expanding Abroad? Avoid Cultural Gaffes," *Wall Street Journal*, January 19, 2010, http://online.wsj.com/news/articles/SB1000142405274870365 7604575005511903147960 (accessed October 15, 2013).

10. Rachel Dodes, "Spanx Body Slimmers for Men Unveiled," *Wall Street Journal*, February 16, 2010, http://blogs.wsj.com/runway/2010/02/16/spanx-body-slimmers -for-men-unveiled/ (accessed October 3, 2013).

11. James Haggerty, "Harley, With Macho Intact, Tries to Court More Women," October 31, 2011, http://online.wsj.com/news/articles/SB10001424052970204505304 576655244217556816 (accessed January 31, 2013).

12. Correen Bailor, Colin Beasty, Marshall Lager, Alexandra DeFelice, "The 2005 CRM Market Leaders, Part 1," *CRM Magazine*, October 2005, http://www.destination crm.com/Articles/Editorial/Magazine-Features/The-2005-CRM-Market-Leaders, -Part-1-41935.aspx (accessed October 3, 2013).

13. Joanne Correia, Yanna Dharmasthira, Chris Pang, "Market Share Analysis: Customer Relationship Management Software, WorldWide, 2012," http://www.gart ner.com/newsroom/id/2459015 (accessed October 3, 2013); Chris Pettey, "Gartner Says Worldwide CRM Total Software Revenue Increased 14 Percent in 2005," *Gartner*, June 12, 2006, http://www.gartner.com/newsroom/id/493005 (accessed January 27, 2014); Louis Columbus, "2013 CRM Market Share Update: 40% of CRM Systems Sold Are SaaS-Based," *Forbes*, April 26, 2013, http://www.forbes.com/sites /louiscolumbus/2013/04/26/2013-crm-market-share-update-40-of-crm-systems -sold-are-saas-based/ (accessed January 27, 2014); Martin Schneider, "CRM License Sales Down 25 Percent in 2002," *CRM Magazine*, June 12, 2003, http://www .destinationcrm.com/Articles/CRM-News/Daily-News/CRM-License-Sales -Down-25-Percent-in-2002-48271.aspx (accessed January 27, 2014); John Ryan, "CRM Market Grew 12.5 Percent Globally in 2008—Gartner," *Ulitzer*, July 16, 2009, http://johnryan.ulitzer.com/node/1038760 (accessed January 27, 2014); "Gartner Says Worldwide CRM New License Revenue Returned to Positive Growth in 2004," *Gartner*, September 12, 2005, http://www.gartner.com/newsroom /id/492191 (accessed January 27, 2012); "Gartner Says Worldwide Customer Relationship Management Market Grew 23 Percent in 2007," *Gartner*, July 7, 2008, http://www.gartner.com/newsroom/id/715308 (accessed January 27, 2014); "Gartner Says Worldwide Customer Relationship Management Software Market Grew 12.5 Percent in 2012," *Gartner*, April 29, 2013, http://www.gartner.com/newsroom /id/2459015 (accessed January 27, 2014); "Salesforce.com—The Best Short Available?" *Seeking Alpha*, November 29, 2010, http://seekingalpha.com/article/238953 -salesforce-com-the-best-short-available (accessed January 27, 2014); Chuck Schaeffer, "Sizing Up the CRM Software Market: The CRM Market for 2013 and Beyond," *CRM Search*, http://www.crmsearch.com/crm-market.php, (accessed January 27, 2014); Coreen Bailor, Colin Beasty, Marshall Lager, Alexandra DeFelice, "The 2005 CRM Market Leaders, Part 1," *CRM Magazine*, October 2005, http://www .destinationcrm.com/Articles/Editorial/Magazine-Features/The-2005-CRM-Mar ket-Leaders,-Part-1-41935.aspx (accessed January 27, 2014).

14. Louis Columbus, "2013 CRM Market Share Update: 40% of CRM Systems Sold are Saas-Based," *Forbes*, April 26, 2013, http://www.forbes.com/sites/louis columbus/2013/04/26/2013-crm-market-share-update-40-of-crm-systems-sold- are-saas-based/ (accessed October 3, 2013).

15. Phil Goldstein, "Report: Skype Makes Up One-Third of All International Phone Traffic," *FierceWireless.com*, February 15, 2013, http://www.fiercewireless.com /story/report-skype-makes-one-third-all-international-phone-traffic/2013-02-15 (accessed October 3, 2013).

16. Eric Pfanner, "Skype Hopes for $100 Million from Initial Offering," *New York Times,* August 9, 2010, http://www.nytimes.com/2010/08/10/technology/10skype .html?hpw&_r=0 (accessed October 3, 2013).

17. Jason Ankeny, "Microsoft Acquires Skype for $8.5B in Cash," *FierceMobileContent. com,* May 10, 2011, http://www.fiercemobilecontent.com/story/microsoft-acquires -skype-85b-cash/2011-05-10 (accessed October 3, 2013).

18. Thomas Derdak, "Iron Mountain Inc.," *Gale Directory of Company Histories,* http:// www.answers.com/topic/iron-mountains-1 (accessed October 3, 2013).

19. Jeff Bussgang, "Scaling is Hard Case Study: Athenahealth," *Inc.,* September 6, 2012, http://www.inc.com/jeff-bussgang/scaling-is-hard-case-study-athenahealth.html (accessed October 7, 2013).

20. Crunchbase, "Athenahealth Profile," *TechCrunch,* September 18, 2013, http://www .crunchbase.com/company/athenahealth (accessed October 8, 2013).

21. CBS MoneyWatch, "Why Mergers Fail," April 12, 2102, http://www.cbsnews .com/8301-505125_162-57411239/why-mergers-fail/ (accessed November 14, 2013).

22. Paul Carroll and Chunka Mui, "Seven Ways to Fail Big," *Harvard Business Review,* September 2008, http://hbr.org/2008/09/seven-ways-to-fail-big/ar/1 (accessed January 19, 2014).

CHAPTER 3: GET MORE COVERAGE

1. Dave Kellogg, "The Self-Fulfilling 3x Pipeline Coverage Prophecy" *Kellblog,* April 19, 2013, http://kellblog.com/2013/04/19/the-self-fulfilling-3x-pipeline-coverage -prophecy (accessed November 15, 2013).

2. Software-as-a-service (SaaS) companies will enjoy David Skok's blog on pipeline management (www.forentrepreneurs.com).

3. Christian Holsthtt, "Fundamental Guidelines of E-Commerce Checkout Design," http://uxdesign.smashingmagazine.com/2011/04/06/fundamental-guidelines-of-e -commerce-checkout-design (accessed November 15, 2013).

4. Ryan Holiday, *Growth Hacking* (New York: Portfolio, 2013), 7.

CHAPTER 4: FIND THE NEXT S-CURVE

1. Ben Dickie, "Cabot Hosiery/Darn Tough Vermont Posts Strongest Year in Company's 34-year History," *PR Web,* January 24, 2013, http://www.prweb.com /releases/2013/1/prweb10341625.htm (accessed October 4, 2013).

2. Joyce Rosenberg, "How Companies Reinvent Themselves," *News-Sentinel.com,* November 19, 2012, http://www.news-sentinel.com/article/2012311199991 (accessed October 4, 2013).

3. Francois Brochet, Suraj Srinivasan, and Michael Norris, "Netflix: Valuing a New Business Model," *Harvard Business School,* January 11, 2013.

4. Peter Cohan, "How Netflix Reinvented Itself," *Forbes,* April 23, 2013, http://www .forbes.com/sites/petercohan/2013/04/23/how-netflix-reinvented-itself/ (accessed October 14, 2013).

5. Matt Hickey, "Netflix to Offer $11.99 Family Plan, Beats HBO in Subscribers," *Forbes,* April 22, 2013, http://www.forbes.com/sites/matthickey/2013/04/22/net flix-to-offer-11-99-family-plan-beats-hbo-in-subscribers/ (accessed October 14, 2013).

6. John Hechinger, "Southern New Hampshire, a Little College That's a Giant Online," *Businessweek,* May 9, 2013, http://www.businessweek.com/articles/2013-05-09

/southern-new-hampshire-a-little-college-thats-a-giant-online (accessed October 14, 2013).

7. Anya Kamenetz, "Most Innovative Companies 2012," *Fast Company*, February 7, 2012, http://www.fastcompany.com/3017340/most-innovative-companies-2012/1 2southern-new-hampshire-university (accessed October 15, 2013).

8. Hechinger, "Southern New Hampshire, a Little College That's a Giant Online."

9. Kamenetz, "Most Innovative Companies 2012."

10. Ibid.

11. Farhad Manjoo, "2012 Most Innovative Companies, Jawbone #18," *Fast Company*, February 7, 2012, http://www.fastcompany.com/3017353/most-innovative-compa nies-2012/18jawbone (accessed October 12, 2013).

12. Sarah Lacy, "Hosain Rahman on Up Jawbone's First Non-Audio Product," *Tech-Crunch*, July 13, 2011, http://techcrunch.com/2011/07/13/hosain-rahman-on-up -jawbones-first-non-audio-product/ (accessed October 12, 2013).

13. Kara Swisher, "Jawbone Hires Microsoft's Mindy Mount as President," *All Things Digital*, May 23, 2013, http://allthingsd.com/20130523/jawbone-hires-microsofts -mindy-mount-as-president/ (accessed October 12, 2013).

14. Pui-Wing Tam, "Jawbone Snags a Heady Valuation," *Wall Street Journal*, July 14, 2011, http://online.wsj.com/news/articles/SB10001424052702304223804576444 063700611644 (accessed October 12, 2013).

15. Gregory Huang, "PackBots, Roombas, and Now, Health Care: The iRobot Story," *Xconomy*, September 12, 2012, http://www.xconomy.com/boston/2012/09/12 /packbots-roombas-and-now-healthcare-the-irobot-story/?single_page=true (ac-cessed October 8, 2013).

16. Neil Hughes, "Apple Accounts for 20% of all 2012 US Consumer Technol-ogy Sales Revenue," *Apple Insider*, February 19, 2013, http://appleinsider.com /articles/13/02/19/apple-accounted-for-20-of-all-2012-us-consumer-technology -sales-revenue (accessed October 12, 2013).

17. Peter Cohan, "Apple's Self-Proclaimed 'Cool' Prompts Stock Drop," *Forbes*, June 11, 2013, http://www.forbes.com/sites/petercohan/2013/06/11/apples-self-proclaimed cool-prompts-stock-drop/ (accessed October 12, 2013).

18. Rip Empson, "As It Moves Beyond Rentals to Become a Student Hub, Chegg Brings 2.5M Textbook Solutions to iOS," *TechCrunch*, January 30, 2013, http://tech crunch.com/2013/01/30/as-it-moves-beyond-rentals-to-become-an-academic-hub -chegg-brings-2-5m-textbook-solutions-to-ios/ (accessed October 10, 2013).

19. Ibid.

20. Miguel Helft, "We Rent Movies, So Why Not Textbooks?," *New York Times*, July 4, 2009, http://www.nytimes.com/2009/07/05/business/05ping.html?_r=1& (ac-cessed October 10, 2013).

21. Helen Coster, "Chegg's New Chapter," *Forbes*, January 25, 2012, http://www.forbes .com/forbes/2012/0213/technology-books-dan-rosensweig-chegg-new-chapter .html (accessed October 10, 2013).

22. Eric Jackson, "An Interview with Dan Rosensweig of Chegg," *Forbes*, February 27, 2013, http://www.forbes.com/sites/ericjackson/2013/02/27/an-interview-with-dan -rosensweig-of-chegg/ (accessed October 10, 2013).

23. Sarah Kessler, "Textbook Renter Chegg Moves Beyond Books," *Mashable*, March 24, 2011, *Mashable*, http://mashable.com/2011/03/24/chegg-social/ (accessed Oc-tober 10, 2013).

24. Eric Jackson, "An Interview with Dan Rosensweig of Chegg," *Forbes*, February 27, 2013, http://www.forbes.com/sites/ericjackson/2013/02/27/an-interview-with-dan -rosensweig-of-chegg/ (accessed October 10, 2013).

25. Quentin Hardy, "H.P.'s Misstep Shows Risk in the Push for Big Ideas," *New York Times,* November 21, 2012, http://www.nytimes.com/2012/11/22/technology/hps -misstep-shows-risk-in-the-push-for-big-ideas.html?ref=business (accessed October 14, 2013).

26. Andy Grove, *Only the Paranoid Survive* (New York: Currency, 1996), 68.

CHAPTER 5: WHAT'S YOUR INNOVATION PROCESS?

1. Austin Carr, "Nike: The No. 1 Most Innovative Company of 2013," *Fast Company,* February 11, 2013, http://www.fastcompany.com/most-innovative-compa nies/2013/nike (accessed October 16, 2013).

2. Bharat Mediratta, "The Google Way: Give Engineers Room," *New York Times,* October 21, 2007, http://www.nytimes.com/2007/10/21/jobs/21pre.html?_r=0 (accessed October 18, 2013).

3. Laura He, "Google's Secrets of Innovation: Empowering Its Employees," *Forbes,* March 29, 2013, http://www.forbes.com/sites/laurahe/2013/03/29/googles-secrets -of-innovation-empowering-its-employees/ (accessed October 18, 2013).

4. Mediratta, "The Google Way: Give Engineers Room."

5. Haydn Shaughnessy, "Google Moonshots: Innovation or Desperation?," July 8, 2013, *Forbes,* http://www.forbes.com/sites/haydnshaughnessy/2013/07/08/googles -moonshots-innovation-or-desperation/ (accessed October 19, 2013).

6. Kara Swisher, "Maybe Googlers Eat Their Own Dog Food, but Will It Be Tasty to Anyone Else?," *AllThingsD,* December 14, 2009, http://allthingsd.com/20091214 /maybe-googlers-eat-their-own-dog-food-but-will-it-be-tasty-to-anyone-else/ (accessed October 18, 2013).

7. Joceyln Hawkes, "Kayak on Creating a Culture of Innovation," *Fast Company,* April 3, 2012, http://www.fastcompany.com/1827003/kayak-creating-culture-innovation (Accessed October 18, 2013).

8. John Camillus, "Strategy as a Wicked Problem," *Harvard Business Review,* May 2008.

9. Tim Brown, "Our Approach: Design Thinking," http://www.ideo.com/about/ (accessed November 16, 2013).

10. Jeanne Liedtka and Tim Ogilvie, *Designing for Growth: A Design Thinking Toolkit for Managers* (New York: Columbia University Press, 2012). 21-37.

11. Hasso Plattner Institute of Design at Stanford, "bootcamp bootleg" 2009, http:// dschool.stanford.edu/wp-content/uploads/2011/03/METHODCARDS2010v6 .pdf (accessed November 20, 2013).

CHAPTER 6: CUSTOMER EXPERIENCE IS THE NEW IP

1. "How Inc. 500 CEOs Innovate," *Inc.*, September 2013, http://www.inc.com/maga zine/201309/how-the-inc.500-companies-innovate.html (accessed October 24, 2013).

2. Micheline Maynard, "Honda Steals the 2013 New York Auto Show with a Vacuum Cleaner," *Forbes,* March 27, 2013, http://www.forbes.com/sites/micheline maynard/2013/03/27/honda-steals-the-2013-new-york-auto-show-with-a-vacuum -cleaner/ (accessed October 24, 2013).

3. "Idea Factories," *Inc.,* September 2013: p. 104.

4. Mark Goulston, telephone conversation with author, October 30, 2013.

5. Clay Christensen, *The Innovator's Solution* (Boston: Harvard Business School Press, 2003), 78.

CHAPTER 7: SOLVE PROBLEMS LIKE A DESIGNER

1. QuoteWorld.org, http://www.quoteworld.org/quotes/9882 (accessed November 15, 2013).
2. *Fast Company* Staff, "Decade in Design: The Biggest Events of 2008," *Fast Company,* October 2013, http://www.fastcodesign.com/3016469/innovation-by-design /decade-in-design-the-biggest-events-of-2008 (accessed October 25, 2013).
3. Eric Markowitz, "Don't Bet Against Aaron Levie," *Inc.,* December 2013: 34.
4. Matthew Panzarino, "This Is How Apple's Top Secret Product Development Process Works," *The Next Web,* January 24, 2012, http://thenextweb.com/apple/2012/01/24 /this-is-how-apples-top-secret-product-development-process-works/ (accessed October 25, 2013).
5. W. Chan Kim and Renée Mauborgne, *Blue Ocean Strategy* (Cambridge: Harvard Business School Press, 2005), 4.
6. Leticia Britos Cavagnaro, Stanford University Design Action Lab, https://novoed .com/designthinking/exercises/308 (accessed August 12, 2013).
7. Kaihan Krippendorff and Ana Maria Rivera, "Building Creative Strategies With Patterns," *Harvard Business Review,* March 2004, http://www.kaihan.net/Building -Creative-Strategies-with-Patterns.pdf (accessed November 20, 2013).

CHAPTER 8: FEEDBACK IS A GIFT

1. Martin Bryant, "10 Great Tech Company Pivots," *The Next Web,* September 13, 2011, http://thenextweb.com/insider/2011/09/13/10-great-tech-company-pivots/ (accessed October 29, 2013).
2. Peter Cohan, "Four Lessons Amazon Learned from Webvan's Flop," *Forbes,* June 17, 2013, http://www.forbes.com/sites/petercohan/2013/06/17/four-lessons-amazon -learned-from-webvans-flop/ (accessed October 29, 2013).
3. Alexandra Alter, "*Wool:* SciFi's Underground Hit," *Wall Street Journal,* March 8, 2013, http://online.wsj.com/news/articles/SB20001424127887324678604578340 752088305668 (accessed October 29, 2013).
4. "How DropBox Got Its First 10 Million Users," *TechCrunch,* November 1, 2011, http://techcrunch.com/2011/11/01/founder-storie-how-dropbox-got-its-first -10-million-users/ (accessed October 29, 2013).
5. Mitch Harper, conversation with author, November 20, 2013.
6. Basheera Khan, "Rapid Prototyping the Google X Way," Mind the Product, December 2, 2013, http://www.mindtheproduct.com/2012/12/rapid-prototyping-the -google-x-way/ (accessed December 1, 2013).
7. Jeanne Liedtka, "Design Thinking for Business Innovation," Coursera, December 2013, https://class.coursera.org/designbiz-001/ (accessed December 1, 2013).
8. John McDermott, "Groupon Pivots Amid Management Upheaval, Lagging Stock Price," *Ad Age,* June 18, 2013, http://adage.com/article/cmo-strategy/groupon -pivots-amid-management-upheaval-lagging-stock-price/242095/ (accessed October 31, 2013); Seth Fiegerman, "Groupon Pivots Further From Daily Deals With Upscale Restaurant Reservations," *Mashable,* http://mashable.com/2013/07/01 /groupon-restaurant-reservations/ (accessed December 1, 2013).
9. Steve Blank, *The Startup Owner's Manual* (Pescadero, CA: K&S Ranch), 2012.
10. "Pinterest CEO: Here's How We Became the Web's Next Big Thing," *Business Insider,* April 2012, http://www.businessinsider.com/pinterest-founding-story-2012-4#this-is -ben-silbermann-the-ceo-of-pinterest-hes-soft-spoken-he-dresses-like-any-old-twenty -something-living-in-san-francisco-or-brooklyn-1 (accessed October 30, 2013).

11. Kara Swisher and Liz Gannes, "Pinterest Does Another Massive Funding—$225 Million at $3.8 Billion," *All Things D,* October 23, 2013, http://allthingsd.com /20131023/pinterest-does-another-massive-funding-225-million-at-3-8-billion -valuation/ (October 30, 2013).
12. Joan Schneider and Julie Hall, "Why Most Product Launches Fail," *Harvard Business Review,* April 2011, http://hbr.org/2011/04/why-most-product-launches-fail /ar/2 (accessed October 31, 2013).

CHAPTER 9: NEW WAYS TO MAKE MONEY

1. www.businessmodelgeneration.com/canvas.
2. Seth Fiegerman, "Apple Has Twice the Sales Per Square Foot of Any Other U.S. Retailer," *Mashable,* November 13, 2012, http://mashable.com/2012/11/13/apple -stores-top-sales-per-square-foot/ (accessed October 31, 2013).

CHAPTER 10: AIR COVER

1. Tom Kelley and David Kelley, *Creative Confidence: Unleashing the Creative Power Within Us All* (New York: Random House, 2013), chapter 2.
2. Ina Fried, "Eric Schmidt on the Demise of Google Wave," *CNET,* August 4, 2010, http://news.cnet.com/8301-13860_3-20012724-56.html (accessed November 7, 2013).
3. Urs Holtzle, Google Blog Post, August 4, 2010, http://googleblog.blogspot.com /2010/08/update-on-google-wave.html (accessed November 7, 2013).
4. Sue Shellenbarger, "Better Ideas Through Failure," *The Wall Street Journal,* September 27, 2011, http://online.wsj.com/news/articles/SB1000142405297020401060 4576594671572584158 (accessed November 7, 2013).
5. Jeff Bezos, "10,000 Year Clock," http://www.10000yearclock.net/learnmore.html (accessed November 7, 2013).
6. ycharts.com (accessed November 7, 2013).
7. Amazon.com, 1997 Annual Report, 1998, http://phx.corporate-ir.net/phoenix .zhtml?c=97664&p=irol-reportsannual (accessed November 7, 2013).
8. Amazon.com, 2006 Annual Report, 2007, http://phx.corporate-ir.net/phoenix .zhtml?c=97664&p=irol-reportsannual (accessed November 7, 2013).
9. George Gradt, "Risk and Reward: Does Your CEO Take the Big Bet?" *Forbes,* May 8, 2013, http://www.forbes.com/sites/georgebradt/2013/05/08/risk-and-reward-does -your-ceo-take-the-big-bet/ (accessed November 8, 2013).
10. Austin Carr, "Inside Netflix's Project Griffin: The Forgotten History Of Roku Under Reed Hastings" *Fast Company,* January 23, 2013.
11. Walter Isaacson, *Steve Jobs* (New York: Simon & Schuster, 2011), 371.
12. David Kaplan, "Howard Schultz Brews Strong Coffee at Starbucks," *Fortune,* November 17, 2011, http://management.fortune.cnn.com/2011/11/17/starbucks -howard-schultz-business-person-year/ (accessed November 7, 2013).
13. George Anders, "Meg Whitman Jolts HP As Its Reluctant Savior," *Forbes,* June 10, 2013, http://www.forbes.com/sites/georgeanders/2013/05/22/meg-whitman-jolts -hp-as-its-reluctant-savior/ (accessed October 20, 2013).

CHAPTER 11: INNOVATION IS NOT A FIRE DRILL

1. Steven Covey, *The 7 Habits of Highly Effective People* (New York: Simon & Schuster, 1989), 102.

2. The Build Network Staff, "Aligned Teams Are All Alike; Every Misaligned Team is Misaligned In Its Own Way," *Inc., Build Quarterly,* November 2013, http://www .inc.com/the-build-network/every-misaligned-team-is-misaligned-in-its-own-way .html.

3. Chip and Dan Heath, *Switch: How to Change Things When Change Is Hard* (New York: Broadway Books, 2010), 76.

SELECTED BIBLIOGRAPHY

Blank, Steve; Dorf, Bob. *The Startup Owner's Manual.* Pescadero, CA: K&S Ranch, 2012.

Christensen, Clay; Raynor, Michael. *The Innovator's Solution.* Boston: Harvard Business School Press, 2003.

Gray, Dave; Brown, Sunni; Macanufo, James. *Gamestorming.* Sebastopol, CA: O"Reilly Media, 2010.

Goulston, Mark. *Just Listen.* New York: AMACOM, 2009.

Harnish, Verne. *Mastering the Rockefeller Habits.* New York: SelectBooks, 2002.

Holiday, Ryan, *Growth Hacker Marketing.* New York: Portfolio, 2013.

Isaacson, Walter. *Steve Jobs.* New York: Simon & Schuster, 2011.

Kelley, Dave; Kelly, Tom. *Creative Confidence.* New York: Crown Business, 2013.

Kim, W. Chan; Mauborgne, Renée. *Blue Ocean Strategy.* Cambridge: Harvard Business School Press, 2005.

Krippendorf, Kaihan, *Hide A Dagger Behind A Smile.* Avon, MA: Adams Media, 2008.

Leidtka, Jeanne; Ogilvie, Tim. *Designing for Growth.* New York: Columbia University Press, 2011.

Levitt, Theodore. *The Marketing Imagination.* New York: The Free Press, 1983.

LUMA Institute. *Innovating for People: Handbook of Human-Centered Design Methods.* Pittsburgh: LUMA Institute, 2012.

Osterwalder, Alexander. *Business Model Generation.* New York: Wiley, 2010.

Moore, Geoffrey. *Crossing the Chasm.* New York: Harper Business, 1991.

Moore, Geoffrey. *Inside the Tornado.* New York: Harper Business, 1995.

Ries, Eric. *The Lean Startup.* New York: Crown Business, 2011.

Nussbaum, Bruce. *Creative Intelligence.* New York: HarperCollins, 2013.

Von Hippel, Eric. *The Sources of Innovation.* New York: Oxford University Press, 1994.

INDEX

8

Another First Day
at School

I didn't mind the taste of this as much as I had the burning whiskey she had given me the night before. Stuart, showing off, drank his bottle in one long gulp, his Adam's apple bobbing like a frog. Nikki and Raspberry clapped and squealed as he reached the end and pulled the bottle out of his mouth.

"Hell, that was nothing," he said. "I can do it with a quart of beer."

"Wow," Nikki said. "A whole quart at once."

"I could probably do more if the bottle was bigger," Stuart bragged.

I saw the girls stifle giggles behind his back when he turned to me.

"You're going to live here now?" he asked.

I nodded.

"I deliver gas to your . . . what is she, your aunt?"